W9-BJH-265

Journey Without Distance

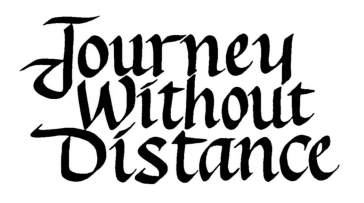

Journey Without Distance

The story behind
A COURSE IN MIRACLES

by Robert Skutch

CELESTIAL ARTS
Berkeley • Toronto

Copyright © 1984 Robert Skutch

All rights reserved. No part of this book may be reproduced or transmitted in any form or by any means, electronic or mechanical, including photo-copying, recording, or by any information storage or retrieval system, except for brief review, without the express permission of the publisher.

Celestial Arts
an imprint of Ten Speed Press
P.O. Box 7123
Berkeley, California 94707
www.tenspeed.com

Cover and book design by Mary Russel, Sausalito, CA
Calligraphy by Patricia Cummins, Greenbrae, CA

ISBN-13: 978-1-58761-108-7
ISBN-10: 1-58761-108-2

Manufactured in the United States of America

14 15—10 09 08

The material from *A Course in Miracles* is used by permission of the copyright owner, Foundation for *A Course in Miracles*, Temecula, CA 92590. The Course, a three-volume hard cover set of books, can be ordered directly from the Foundation for Inner Peace for $40.00. The single-volume edition is also available from the Foundation for $28.00 softcover or $30.00 hardcover.

On behalf of all who have benefited by studying *A Course in Miracles*, this book is lovingly dedicated to Helen, Bill, Ken and Judy

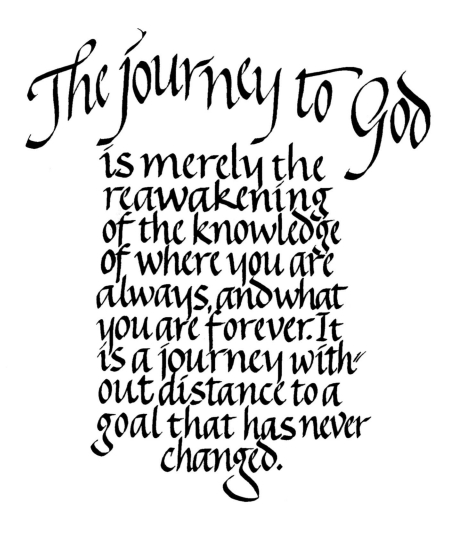

The journey to God is merely the reawakening of the knowledge of where you are always, and what you are forever. It is a journey without distance to a goal that has never changed.

A COURSE IN MIRACLES

Foreword

A couple of years ago I casually remarked to a man who was interviewing me that I thought the set of books entitled *A Course in Miracles* comprise perhaps the most important writing in the English language since the translation of the Bible. I went on to explain my reasoning, that although the Course deals with the same discoverable psychological and spiritual truths as the New Testament, it presents them in a form that is harder to evade—because it is more specific and less liable to various interpretations, and also because the psychospiritual exercises employed are so effective in helping us elude our normal defenses against self-discovery I did not expect my impulsive statement to appear in print, but it did. In retrospect, I think that casual though it was, I would stand by it.

My own introduction to the Course came after a quarter of a century of search. Trained in physics and electrical engineering, and impressed with the power of science, I was dubious of most of the religious approaches I encountered which appeared to necessitate suspension of what seemed to me a healthy scientific skepticism. In 1954, at age 36, an "up-ending" experience in the form of an intensive two-week seminar had initiated a quest which by age 59 had brought me in contact with numerous paths—Zen to Sufism to Vedanta to mystical Christianity—and also with a series of experiences which were totally astonishing to me since my conceptual framework had no place for their likes. The experiences felt valid, and the spiritual philosophies had the ring of truth about them; still, there was a missing factor Furthermore, I was vaguely aware that if the experiences were as veridical as I felt them to be, and the philosophies as true, they should be affecting my life more than they were.

At that point, I had moved from statistical communications theory and systems analysis to heading up a small group at Stanford Research Institute doing research on social change and future-oriented planning. After ten years of futures research I had published a small book entitled *An Incomplete Guide to the Future,* the existence of which was one of the better kept secrets in publishing history It was clear to me by then that the United States, and indeed the industrialized world, had entered a transition period of historic significance, involving change at the most fundamental level—namely, the basic tacitly agreed upon premises about the nature of life and reality upon which the whole structure of society ultimately rests. It seemed that, whereas half a century earlier the advance of positivistic science was making the religious/spiritual assumptions steadily less plausible, the picture was now otherwise. By 1977, and even more so in the years since, research into the mysteries of human consciousness, unconscious processes, intuition and creativity, etc., were progressively making the essential spirituality of existence more plausible. Impressed with the importance of this development, I agreed to serve on the Board of the Institute of Noetic Sciences, founded several years earlier by Apollo 14 astronaut Edgar Mitchell, who had reached similar conclusions to mine through dramatically different experiences. One of my fellow board members was Judith Skutch.

When we first met. we were waiting for a restaurant table, and I asked Judy the inevitable getting-acquainted question, "What do you do?" She enjoyed my astonished look as she replied, "A Course in Miracles." For the next two hours I sat spellbound as she related the story told in this book. I couldn't wait to get my hands on the three books which make up *A Course in Miracles.*

I had much to learn about the ambivalence with which we humans approach getting acquainted with our deeper selves. The daily exercises in affirming a new belief system, which comprise the second volume of the Course, seemed simple and mildly intriguing; I had no understanding at the time of the subterranean effect they were having. The Text, the first volume, seemed abstruse, but I went at it with a will (I thought). Six months later I was shocked to realize that in spite of opening the Text daily, I could not recall ever finishing a single page. I would get sleepy; my mind would wander;

I would remember tasks undone and would get up to do them. My mind was most ingenious at avoiding that which I thought I wanted—namely, understanding the contents of the Text.

In time, the conscious intention won out over the unconscious resistance. My awareness that this was the case came in small steps. One day I would realize that a situation which once would have aroused fear or hostility no longer did so—and yet I would have had no conscious awareness of the deep-seated changes taking place. I would find that my trust in a deep intuition, an all-knowing and all-forgiving part of myself, had strengthened noticeably, again without my direct conscious knowledge of the change taking place in the unconscious part of my mind. Stress and pain disappeared. My life was more active than at any previous period, and yet it happened more effortlessly than I would have been able to believe possible in earlier years. Aspects of my life fell into place in ways that were nothing short of mysterious. What impressed me most about the transformation I felt was the utter simplicity of the new way A deeper part of myself, an "Inner Teacher," guided action and removed obstacles, and the conscious mind—that rational, analytical ego-mind which once seemed my best precarious hold on some semblance of security—became naturally and comfortably the servant of the deeper mind. It will likely sound like a gross over-simplification, but my deeply felt conclusion came to be that all the problems we experience in our lives are illusory There is only one problem, namely our resistance to seeing things as they truly are, or more accurately, seeing the wholeness as it is.

A Course in Miracles has by now influenced hundred of thousands of lives. I feel privileged to have known Helen Schucman and Bill Thetford and the other players in the drama—not well, all of them, but well enough to have experienced a deep sense of mystery, not only about the efficacy of the Course itself, but also about the way in which it came and about its presumed source. I recall especially one day when I was discussing the Course with Helen, who still felt somewhat ambivalent about it, and seemed somehow not fully able to adapt its insight into her own life. Suddenly she seemed to transform into another person—not visually so much, as in terms of personality For a minute or two, for a few sentences, this "other" Helen spoke of the real meaning of the Course with an authenticity and deep wisdom that left me awestruck. Then, as if by another flick of an inner switch, she was the ordinary Helen again.

Helen hardly seemed to embody the inner peace that the Course puts forth as its goal. She found much to complain about, and her life seemed to contain more than the usual amount of pain. I once asked her how it happened that this remarkable document she had been responsible for had brought wisdom and peace to so many, and yet it was seemingly ineffective for her I will never forget her reply "I *know* the Course is true, Bill," she said—and then after a pause, "but I don't believe it."

When it began to be apparent that *A Course in Miracles* was spreading rapidly, even to other countries, I felt keenly the need to have an accurate account of its origin available to the many who would eventually want to know It seemed likely that myths might circulate, and that even Helen might be made into some sort of cult heroine. I urged that an accurate history be assembled while memories were still fresh, and that the writing be done by someone close to the events, but not too close. Bob Skutch, I felt, was the ideal candidate. He had watched at least the latter portion of the story unfold. he knew all the characters personally and they were available to him for interviews; thus he could tell the story with fidelity concerning the people and events involved; furthermore, he had done some previous professional writing. Needless to say, when asked he agreed. While he may not have always felt thankful for my suggestion, nevertheless he was gracious enough to invite me to write this foreword.

I am grateful for the honor because I believe *A Course in Miracles* will one day be much more widely appreciated, as will the story of its remarkable genesis.

Willis W Harman Ph.D
Regent, State of California
November 1983
Stanford, California

Two years later he was graduated from eighth grade, and went on to high school where he graduated with honors, and was accepted as a freshman at DePauw University in Indiana. When, as a sophmore he had to elect a subject to major in, he chose psychology, although he really didn't know why, since he wasn't quite sure what psychologists did, and was certainly not convinced he wanted to be one. As a result, he also enrolled in the premedical program—since he *did* know what doctors did—and in his senior year he applied for, and was accepted in the fall term at the University of Chicago Medical School.

Since he had been deferred from military service because of his severe childhood illness he was able to graduate from DePauw in February of 1944. Although he was still uncertain as to what kind of a career he might choose, he was unequivocally clear about one thing· he needed a job in order to support himself—at least until he began medical school in the fall.

Since I had been accepted at the medical school, I thought the best thing to do would be to apply for a job at the University. I inquired at the employment office, and was referred to the University's metallurgical laboratory. I did not know what kind of jobs they might have to offer—or why I might be qualified to hold one— but during my job interview I did learn that the metallurgical laboratory was the center for some sort of classified research program at the University.

Since the country was in the middle of World War II, and civilian manpower was at a premium, people like myself although inexperienced and unqualified, were sought after in the job market, and often given responsibilities they ordinarily would not have assumed. In my case, shortly after I began work I was put on the faculty payroll as an administrative officer, responsible for overseeing a number of buildings which were essential testing areas for what I eventually learned was atomic research. These included the biological science laboratory, the West Stands football stadium area and the new chemistry building where Dr Glenn Seaborg was conducting his original research which later won him a Nobel Prize. One of my special assignments was to be in charge of a special crew of men who went through various radioactive areas and tried to decontaminate them. I was required to wear a Geiger counter from the time I arrived in the morning until I left at night. One of the curious aspects in retrospect, was that all of this research activity took place under the football stadium. Robert Maynard Hutchens, President of the University, had decreed that intercollegiate football was taboo, since it interfered with the pursuit of the great ideas and the great books. As a result, the football stadium had been made available for atomic research. Consequently, the first chain reaction in the history of the world took place there in December 1942. Dr Enrico Fermi was in charge of that experiment, and he was able to both start the reaction and, more importantly, to stop it. If he had not been able to do this perhaps we would all have been spared the horrifying problems ushered in by the atomic age.

The atmosphere in our department at the time was an extremely exciting one. There was a sense of utmost urgency and a high sense of national priority to the work being done in the program. It was the belief of the scientific community that the Nazis had already progressed very far in the development of atomic energy, and that we were in a life or death race with them. It was felt, in fact, that if we did not develop atomic energy first, it could mean the end of Western civilization as we knew it.

During this time my ambivalence about entering medical school continued to grow, and by the fall of 1944 I decided that the project with which I was involved had a higher priority than the study of medicine. I therefore informed the medical school I would not be matriculating that fall, and I continued in my position with the atomic research program.

In August 1945 the first atomic bomb was dropped on Hiroshima. I think all of us were aghast at the extent of the devastation, and I felt clearly that my participation on the project had come to an end. Since I no longer felt a moral commitment to continue, I resigned that same month.

A few weeks later Dr Carl Rogers arrived on campus. Although I knew nothing about Rogers, who even then was one of the most eminent names in the field of psychology, I signed up for his first course on Client Centered Psychotherapy, simply because some of the graduate students I knew recommended that I do so. The interest in Rogers' work was tremendous, and there must have been over a hundred graduate students who took that first course he taught.

For reasons which are as obscure to me now as they were then, Rogers decided I was an advanced graduate student, and not only made me a teaching instructor in this course, but before the end of the quarter invited me to be his research assistant at the counseling center which he had just formed. This was a tremendous honor and opportunity; I did not understand it, and even tried to tell him that I wasn't qualified, but he paid no attention, and, with some bewilderment, I shortly found myself involved in both the research and the practice of client centered psychotherapy. Even more ironic to me was the fact that Rogers' professional premises were founded on his theory of "unconditional positive regard," or perfect love. And for me to have gone directly from being involved with total annihilation to a professional practice based on perfect love seemed, to say the least, ironical.

My doctoral dissertation involved an early attempt at something like biofeedback. I was intrigued with the possibility of measuring the autonomic nervous system and its functions before and after Rogerian psychotherapy. It seemed to me that if people benefited from therapy, they might recover more rapidly from some experimentally induced stress. So I formed a control group of people who were waiting to be accepted at the center for counseling, and a group of people who were actively involved in the counseling process. Somehow the measurements that I used did reveal a significant difference between the experimental and control groups in the rapidity of recovery from the induced stress. Rogers was very impressed by this study, and I was rather stunned that I had actually found any significant results at all.

In March 1949, somewhat to my surprise, I received my Ph.D. However, I still had no real awareness of the field of psychology. Something seemed to be missing although I could not specify what. Although I had met many eminent people during my studies who were authorities in their respective fields, no one seemed to have any awareness of how these specialized areas of knowledge could be synthesized.

As a result, when I received my Ph.D I felt thoroughly unqualified for practically anything, and I wasn't at all sure what one was supposed to do with this degree. Luckily, a friend suggested that I apply for a position at Michael Reese Hospital in Chicago where an opening had occurred in a large project dealing with the study of personality features in schizophrenic patients and the Rorschach test. The study was under the direction of Dr Samuel J. Beck, the leading authority on the Rorschach in this country, who had written pioneering books on the test.

5

For some reasons which seemed perfectly valid to me, I was most reluctant to apply for this position. One was I had never taken a course on the Rorschach in my life; I knew absolutely nothing about it. Also, I had never worked in a department of psychiatry, particularly one which emphasized psychoanalysis—a philosophy totally contrary to that of Rogers'and my own background However, I did apply, and Dr Beck, who interviewed me, seemed very pleased by my lack of qualifications. First he expressed extreme enthusiasm over the fact that I knew nothing about the Rorschach and was obviously uncontaminated by other teachings. Second, he was most impressed with the scientific sounding title of my doctoral dissertation, which was in the area of physiological psychology. And since he knew nothing at all about this area, he thought it was extremely scientific, and that I therefore was the perfect candidate. I was hired in the department of psychiatry, and stayed at Michael Reese for two and a half years, publishing a number of research papers, including several which I co-authored with Dr Beck.

The one thing I felt strongly about, both during graduate studies and afterwards at Michael Reese, was that I did not in any way wish to be a university professor I had made a secret vow with myself that I would do everything possible to avoid accepting any professorial position, and I had already turned down several offers. One of the chief reasons for my feelings about not wanting to be a professor was that I felt I had nothing to profess, and was unwilling to put myself in a position where this might become apparent to others. Also, I did not feel that university life was something that I would happily adapt to.

When I felt it was time to move on from the hospital, I decided it would be instructive and helpful to go to Washington, D C. and enroll in the Washington School of Psychiatry. The essential philosophy of the Washington School was to focus on interpersonal relations rather than upon many of the psychodynamic components of Freudian psychology. This appealed to me a great deal, since I felt there was a quality in psychoanalysis that I could not identify with, even though I respected many of the insights made by Freud and some of his followers.

When I completed the study program at the Washington School, I was undecided about what to do next. Since I had long been attracted to New York City I decided to go there and look for a position. The head of the Psychological Placement Service at the N.Y

State Employment Service said he had absolutely the perfect job for me, and that there was no point in my even thinking about any other position. What he had in mind was the Directorship of the Psychology Department at the Institute of Living in Hartford, Connecticut. I went there for an interview and was hired.

After a year at Hartford I received a call from Dr Harold G. Wolff, one of the founders of psychosomatic medicine, a leading authority on stress disorders, and at the time Chairman of the Department of Neurology at Cornell University Medical College in New York City. Dr Wolff offered me an appointment as Chief Psychologist in the Human Ecology Study Program which he was directing. My uneasiness about becoming involved in a university position had mellowed somewhat by this time and I decided to consider an academic appointment. As a result, I accepted Dr Wolff's offer, and before I knew it I became an instructor and a year later I was promoted to assistant professor

One day in the fall of 1957 I was attending an annual psychological meeting, and during one of the breaks an old friend of mine came up to me and after the usual amenities asked me if I would be interested in coming to Columbia University's College of Physicians and Surgeons to head a pre-doctoral training program in clinical psychology. He said it was an extremely challenging position and the search committee had not been able to agree on anyone to fill it. He indicated that many candidates had been considered, but each one had been vetoed by one or more members of the committee, and so the position had remained unfilled. He said that since no one on the committee knew me well enough to dislike me that I would be the ideal person for the appointment.

I indicated to my friend that I had no real interest in leaving Cornell, for I found my work there quite fascinating, and the atmosphere very pleasant. He did urge me, however, to at least speak to the Chairman of the Psychiatry Department at Columbia, as he felt the opportunity was too unusual to simply ignore.

I did talk to the Chairman, as well as to other people on the search committee, and in the course of these conversations it became apparent that I was being offered an extremely responsible job. Realizing this, I said I didn't think I could possibly assume the responsibilities of that position if I were just an assistant professor, and that I would have to be promoted to associate professor I said this because I was convinced that in the medical hierachy, which moves very slowly, it was most unlikely that someone who

7

had just been an instructor a year or two before would be promoted that quickly.

About two months later, however, I received a letter from the Chairman of the Psychiatry Department who had somehow been able to get my appointment through the Dean's office. As a result I felt morally committed to accepting the appointment, and I went to Columbia in February 1958 as an Associate Professor of Medical Psychology in the Department of Psychiatry at the College of Physicians and Surgeons. ✍

Bill Thetford looked forward to the challenge of his new position with a great deal of enthusiasm. He felt he could introduce a number of innovative ideas into the pre-doctoral training program which he was to head and he took up his duties filled with anticipation of what could be accomplished in the months and years ahead.

Only a few days after he began his new duties, however, Bill began to realize that his job was not going to be as easy to implement as he had originally thought. He got the first hint of this when he realized that all of the discussions he'd had with the various members of the search committee had not really prepared him for the nature and extent of the responsbilities he now faced. Whereas he had believed that most of his time would be devoted to the pre-doctoral program, he now discovered that the additional title he had casually been assigned "as a formality" when he accepted the position—that of Director of the Psychology Department of Presbyterian Hospital— was going to involve much more than he had been led to believe. Presbyterian Hospital was an essential part of the Medical Center, and what Bill learned almost immediately was that along with his "casual title" there also went a host of problems which had not been dealt with for many years.

As he was trying to sort out his priorities, Bill received word from the Dean of the College that the University had accepted a large sum of money from the National Institute of Neurological Diseases to do a cooperative study program on neurological and sensory deficits in infants and young children. This collaborative program had a mandatory protocol which required the services of an experienced research psychologist who had specialized training in working with and testing infants and young children. It became Bill's responsibility to find such a person to fill the position, and to do so quickly, for the Dean had made it quite clear that the project had to be started immediately

Since this was an area in which he had no expertise, he arranged to see a colleague from a neighboring hospital who was one of the authorities in the field. Bill described the situation and asked if his friend could help him find a suitable person for the position. His colleague assured him that he was confident the right person could be found and he would have that person get in touch with Bill.

Bill felt gratified that he had one less problem to deal with, since there seemed to be no dearth of problems for him already So he began to formulate plans and set up procedures that would help the program get off to a smooth start, simply trusting that his friend would indeed find the right person to fill the critical spot.

About two weeks later, the phone rang in Bill's office, and after establishing that she was talking to Dr Thetford, the voice at the other end of the line said, "My name is Dr Helen Schucman, and I was told to tell you that I am the person you are looking for" That was Bill's introduction to Helen with whom he later worked in taking down the remarkable volumes called *A Course in Miracles.*

Bill made an appointment to have Helen come to the Medical Center the next morning for an interview At 10 AM a very small, but dynamic woman in her late forties was ushered into his office. Helen, who was little more than five feet tall, was attractively dressed in a conservative skirt and blouse, and her short, curly, blonde streaked hair was neatly groomed. Her features were rather sharp, with a small angular nose, and she had a no-nonsense attitude about her that immediately struck Bill as being a positive characteristic that he felt would be of great benefit if she were to take the job that he was trying to fill.

After only a few minutes Bill knew she was the right person for the position. Her professional background was made to order for the work that had to be done, and he was especially impressed by her quick mind and intellectual ability At the same time, he was reluctant to offer her—or anyone—the job, for the specifics of the whole program were still extremely nebulous. No decisions had been made as to physical facilities and office space; the salary for the particular position she would be taking had not been agreed on; and the responsibilities of the job were not clearly defined. Therefore, Bill could not be very specific in his discussion of the program with Helen. Despite all this, and despite the fact that Bill gave her a kind of reverse sales pitch, Helen accepted the position and she agreed to begin the following Monday

Chapter 2

Helen Schucman, whose maiden name was Helen Cohn, was born on July 14, 1909. She was raised in New York City, where even during the Great Depression years of the early 1930's, her father, a highly successful chemist, was able to provide the family with an unusually comfortable way of life. This included the services of a cook and a maid to help take care of the ten-room apartment which they occupied, as well as the employment of a governess who took care of Helen until she was six years old.

The governess and Helen lived in one end of the apartment where they shared a bedroom, sitting room and bath. At the other end of the apartment lived the rest of the family This included her mother, father and a brother, who had little in common with a sister who was fourteen years younger than he.

Since the rest of the family seemed to have lives of their own, Helen spent almost all her time prior to entering school, as well as most of her "free time" after entering first grade, with her governess, a middle-aged English lady whom she simply knew as "Miss Richardson." Although Helen and Miss Richardson were on friendly terms, their relationship was anything but intimate; what Helen liked most about Miss Richardson was listening to her English accent.

At night, her governess was officially finished with her job when she had put Helen to bed for the night. After that Miss Richardson was free to go out for the evening, though she mostly remained in the sitting room until she herself went to bed. When Miss Richardson did go out at night, Helen would stay awake until she was sure her governess had returned. She not only wanted to be sure she would not be alone, but she was also fascinated by the ritual that Miss Richardson performed each night.

↬ Before Miss Richardson got into bed, she would kneel down and sort of whisper to herself for a while. She had done this ever since I could first remember I always wanted to ask her about this, but it took a number of years before I got up enough courage to do so. Miss Richardson explained that she was a Catholic, and every night before she went to bed she said the rosary. I asked her what a rosary was and she showed me hers. It was made of pretty blue beads and I liked it. I thought it would probably be a good thing to have, and might even be a little magical. I asked Miss Richardson if I could have one too, but she said it was only for Catholics. I suggested that perhaps my mother would buy one for me, but Miss Richardson thought it would be better not to mention it. In fact, she said it could be our secret, and so I promised not to say anything about it.

She and I had another secret too. This one had to do with where we went on Sunday mornings. Instead of going to the park, as we generally did, we went way over to the other side of the city so that nobody would see us. Then we went to one of the most beautiful places I had ever seen. Miss Richardson told me it was a Catholic church, but since I was not a Catholic I was not allowed to go inside. I had to promise not to wander off, and I stayed inside the hallway until Miss Richardson came out again. While I was waiting though, I could see the flowers and the candles and the statues through the little space between the two large swinging doors that opened into the church. Sometimes I heard music, and a man's voice saying things I did not understand. Once I sneaked around to a little chapel on the side of the church. There was a statue of a lovely lady there, with light around her head and flowers and candles in the little garden in front of her Everyone there had beads like Miss Richardson's rosary, and I made up my mind that when I grew up I would be a Catholic so I could go inside and be part of what Miss Richardson was doing.

On weekdays, when Miss Richardson took me to the park to play, we always met a friend of hers who was a governess too, and who took care of another little girl about my own age. We used to play together while Miss Richardson and her friend sat on a bench together and talked. The little girl, I discovered, was a Catholic. She had a rosary, and was very much surprised when I told her I did not have one and did not know what it was for She explained, rather condescendingly, that it was a prayer to the Mother of God. I asked her about God, and she was really shocked at my ignorance. I knew almost nothing about Him. She told me that God is our Father, and we could ask Him for things and He would give them to us. This sounded pretty wonderful to me, and I wondered why nobody had told me about all this before.

I asked the little girl where God was, because there were quite a few things I wanted. She said that all you had to do was close your eyes and you could see Him. I closed my eyes, but I did not see anything. The little girl had no trouble understanding this; I was not a Catholic, so what could I expect? She suggested that I might try the Blessed Virgin, who was very kind and would listen to practically anyone. She told me that the Blessed Virgin wore a blue dress and a white veil, and I thought of the beautiful statue I had seen in Miss Richardson's church. I closed my eyes again and did a little better this time; I thought I caught a glimpse of a white veil. The little girl said that was very good for a beginner, and I should keep trying. 'After all,' she said, 'unless you do, you'll go to hell and burn forever and ever '

I was so excited about the white veil that I paid no attention to her last remark until I was in bed that night. Then I started to scream. Miss Richardson asked what was the matter, and I told her I was afraid of hell   that I was going to burn forever unless I was a Catholic and had a rosary. Miss Richardson was really concerned, but she had no idea what to say. Finally she told me that I had better ask my parents about religion. She explained that people generally have the same religion as their parents, and that probably they could tell me about things. She added that I need not be afraid of hell, though, because she would pray for me. I thanked her very much, made her promise not to forget and then decided to ask my parents about my religion right away.

I crept down the long hall to the living room where my father was sitting alone reading a newspaper I watched him from the doorway for quite a while before I went inside. Father looked up and seemed surprised.

'Is anything the matter?' he asked. 'Isn't Miss Richardson in?' When I told him she was, he said, 'Oh; well, your mother isn't here, and I don't think she'll be back for a while.' He picked up his newspaper, and seemed to think the conversation was over But I hung around. I did not know him very well and was uncertain how to begin, but I knew I had to find out about my religion. At last I began.

'Father, what are you?' I asked.

'I don't think I understand,' he answered, evidently puzzled. 'Do you mean you want to know what I do?'

I said maybe that was it. My father said he was a chemist. When I asked him to explain that, I didn't understand what he was saying. But I did know it was not the answer I wanted. So I asked him if he believed in God and had a religion. He said he did not believe in God, and was not particularly interested in religion. I asked him if that meant I had no religion either, and he answered that people should decide that for themselves. I asked him what my mother had decided, and he said he was not quite sure what her religion was at the moment. It was evident he was not particularly interested in the subject. Nevertheless I kept hanging around. Finally, when he saw I really had something on my mind, he put down his newspaper and asked me to sit down, after which we had perhaps the only real talk we ever had.

I began by telling him that I wanted to be a Catholic on account of hell. My father replied that he did not believe in hell himself, and did not think I really had to worry. He indicated you could even be religious and not believe in hell, which was a great relief to me. Father said he himself had been Jewish when he was a little boy, because his father was Jewish, and although his mother was not, she had not minded. I asked him, hopefully, if maybe that made me Jewish too, but he only answered that he thought I should think about it for a while. Then I asked if he knew any Jewish prayers. He thought for what seemed like quite a few minutes, and then recited one which he said he had learned when he was a little boy. It began, 'Lord God of Israel,' and I was very much impressed. He said more of the prayer, but that was all I remembered.

I asked him then to tell me some more about my mother's religion, but he said he couldn't keep up with what she believed, and he had stopped trying long ago. When I asked him if maybe she would decide to be Jewish too, my father laughed louder than I had ever heard him; he told me it was not likely. And with that he went back to his newspaper

I went back to my end of the apartment, and told Miss Richardson that I had talked with my father, and had found out I was Jewish. Miss Richardson said nothing at all. That night, however, while she said her rosary, I said 'Lord God of Israel' over and over to myself. I was very excited about being Jewish. I had suspected for a long time that there was something missing about me, and now that I was Jewish I was convinced everything would be all

14

right   I did not mention my religion to my mother, though, somehow I felt she might not like it.

Miss Richardson left about a year later, and my mother decided I did not need a special governess any more. I had been going to school for almost a year now, and my mother said she would take me herself in the mornings, and that a new lady would pick me up in the afternoons and take me to the park, although she would not be sleeping in with me.

It was lonely at night without Miss Richardson. I used to lie in the dark and say my Special Prayer, but it did not help much. I thought it might turn out better, perhaps, if I learned the rest of it. But somehow I did not want to ask my father about it again. He might think I should have remembered it the first time, after he had gone to so much trouble to remember it for me.

And then the Lord God of Israel let me down in a terrible way. I got afraid of sleeping by myself at night, especially when my parents went out. It never occurred to me to go and talk to my brother, and so I found a way to make my mother stay home. If I saw her getting ready to go out, I developed a terrible stomach ache. The first time this happened it was really true. and that is how I discovered my mother would not go out if I were sick. Naturally, I began having lots of stomach aches.

The only trouble was that my mother took me to the doctor to try and find out what was wrong with me. When the first doctor could find nothing, she tried a second. And then a third. I didn't mind, because I got to spend that time with my mother But then one day, when my mother was taking me to see someone else about my stomach, I noticed she was carrying a small suitcase. When I asked her why, she told me I was going to the hospital where a doctor would be able to cure my stomach aches. I had a feeling things were not going the way I wanted them to go, but since I wasn't sure, I remained silent.

When we checked into the hospital, Mother told me I would be spending the night there, and that she would remain with me. I liked that part.

But the next morning Mother and the doctor started to explain what was going to be done. It was then I panicked. In between screams I told them I had never really had any stomach aches, but obviously they thought I was saying that because I was scared of what was going to be done to me—and my appendix.

It took two men in white to hold me down on the table as I was

15

wheeled to the operating room where three other men in white were waiting. Two of the men held me while the third put a mask over my face. I screamed 'Lord God of Israel' over and over, while I tried not to breathe.

When I woke up I was back in my hospital room feeling terrible. I had a real stomach ache for a few days, but after a while I began to feel better and even started to enjoy myself. My mother stayed with me all the time, and even Father came to visit me. Mother and I talked about all sorts of things while we were together, and the evening before we left the hospital, I asked her about her religion. She said she had tried many religions ever since she was little, that she was now a Theosophist, but that she was still 'searching.' I was very surprised to learn she had once been mostly Jewish herself, for she did not seem to like Jews very much. She told me that her father was a rabbi in England, but had come from a very good family anyway. She also said she had some relatives who were not Jewish, and that seemed to be of some help to her

Meanwhile I had decided not to be Jewish any more after what had happened. Probably there was no Lord God of Israel after all, which was why my father had stopped believing in him. I never really believed in God again, although I tried very hard for a long time. ✍

Helen did not have much interest in—or many anxieties about—religion for the next five or six years. What did seem to intrigue her much more were the mental pictures she so often had—sometimes with her eyes closed, other times with them open. They would occur virtually at any time, but they never interrupted or even disturbed her overt activities in any way It was merely as if there was a constant mental activity going on in the background which would be brought more to the foreground if she chose to notice it. The pictures could be of anything: a woman with a dog; trees in the rain; a store window filled with shoes; a birthday cake with lighted candles. The pictures were motionless and in black and white, appearing much like a series of unrelated "stills." Sometimes the pictures were completely new to her—scenes she could not recognize. Other times she would recognize a part of a picture as related to things she had actually seen, but even in those cases there were details which she had no recollection of having seen originally

Helen had been having these mental images ever since she could remember, and it never occurred to her that everyone was not able to enjoy the same experience. In fact, it wasn't until she was eleven years old, when she asked a friend about *her* pictures that she learned that the friend did not have any idea as to what Helen was talking about. Helen thought the friend was teasing her, and it wasn't until she checked with other classmates that she learned that her ability was unique. Although she was quite surprised to learn this, she did not seem to be bothered by the revelation, and she simply went on enjoying her mental pictures whenever they happened to come along.

Helen's concern with God and religion was re-kindled when she was in her twelfth year. Her parents planned to spend the summer in Europe, and they decided to take her with them. The trip was uneventful for Helen until the last stop of their vacation—Lourdes.

The grotto made a deep impression on her, as did the statue of the Blessed Virgin and the piles of used crutches and braces that had been left there by those who had been healed.

From our hotel room I could see the statue of the Blessed Virgin. Every evening I went out to look at the statue, and the rock on which it stood, and the special water that came out of the side of the rock—the water that helped heal people. And I thought about the crutches and the braces and about all the thousands of people who came here and believed. Could all of them be wrong?

I suddenly remembered Miss Richardson and her rosary. Of all the places in the world, this was surely the best one for buying a rosary and trying it out.

When I returned to the hotel that night I found my father alone in his room reading a book. I stood near him a few moments, and when he kept on reading, I told him I wanted to buy a rosary. He put his hand in his pocket and gave me some money without even looking up from his book. I thought about asking him if he minded, but instead I simply said thank you and left the room.

The next morning I asked Mother to come with me to buy the rosary. I also bought a little medal of the Blessed Virgin, and we took them both to a priest to have them blessed. We stayed in the grotto for Mass and for a beautiful service afterwards. It was Saturday, and there were even more flowers and music processions than usual. People were praying everywhere. It was all very, very beautiful. I asked my mother if she had ever been a Catholic, and she said she had not. But I felt she had started thinking about it.

That night in my room I stayed up in the dark with my rosary in my hand and my medal around my neck, and I thought about God and Miss Richardson and the Blessed Virgin. Suddenly I had an idea. This was a wonderful place, and perhaps if I asked for a miracle for myself I would get it. And then I would believe in God and become a Catholic. I went out onto the balcony and looked over to the rock.

'Please, God,' I said aloud, 'I'm not a Catholic, but if all of this is true, would you send me a miracle so I can believe in you?'

I had already decided what the miracle should be. I would close my eyes and say three Hail Marys; if there was a meteor in the sky when I opened my eyes, that would be my miracle. I did not really expect to find the meteor, but I closed my eyes and said three Hail Marys anyway. When I opened my eyes again the sky was full of shooting stars. I watched in stunned silence, and then whispered, 'It's my miracle. God really did send it. Look, oh look! It's my miracle.'

I stood quite still until the stars had faded away and the sky was dark again. And then I remembered. Our guide had told us that this was the time of year for meteor showers in this part of the world, and they would be appearing quite often. It was not really a miracle at all. I had never seen a meteor shower before, and that was why I had not recognized it right away. Then I had another thought. Couldn't it be a miracle that I thought of asking for a meteor just before a meteor shower was due? After all, I had no way of knowing one was coming just then. Maybe it was a real miracle after all. But I could not quite talk myself into it again. I had become deeply suspicious of the whole thing. I even got a little bit angry about it.

Perhaps, I thought to myself, the water and the healings and the crutches were all like the meteor shower People just thought they were miracles. It all could happen like that. I was about to settle it that way when another thought came that made me seriously uncomfortable. I had told God that if I saw a meteor when I opened my eyes it would be my miracle. If there was a God, He might not like the way I was taking His miracle. If God had taken the trouble to send a miracle especially for me, He might not take kindly to all this skepticism. And if there was a God, then there might also be *a hell for people who did not appreciate Him.*

*I finally argued my way out of the situation, although I did re-
main somewhat uneasy about it. I persuaded myself that if God
was going to bother sending me a miracle at all, He would surely
have sense enough to make me believe in it. Since I did not really
believe in this one, it could not have been a genuine miracle.
Anyway, I decided, I did not have to make up my mind definitely
about it right then and there. I would think it all through later
when I wasn't so tired.* ᔕᔕ

A year after they returned from the European trip, Helen's brother
got married, and the family then moved to a smaller apartment.
Idabel, the housekeeper who had been with the family since before
Helen was born, went with them. She and Helen had been good
friends for several years, but the new living situation helped them
become much closer, and they would spend a great deal of time talking about "things." One of the "things" they finally got around to
discussing was religion. Idabel was a Baptist, and she told Helen that
although her church officially believed in hell, she felt God was really
friendly, and arranged things so they always came out all right in the
end. This sounded quite reassuring to Helen, who then began to read
the Bible every evening with Idabel.

One Sunday Idabel asked Helen if she would like to accompany
her to her church, which was quite a way up town from where they
were living. Helen was extremely enthusiastic about the idea, and
when they arrived, she was very anxious for the service to begin.

The people in Idabel's church not only had a different skin color
than Helen, but they also sang songs that were very different from
anything Helen had ever heard before. They sang them over and
over again, beginning softly and getting louder and louder each
time. When the people began clapping their hands and stamping
their feet to the music, Helen knew just how wonderful they were
feeling. But the thing that impressed her most was that she could tell
from the way these people were singing and chanting that they obviously were on very friendly terms with God.

ᔕᔕ *I had always addressed God formally, with great respect, and
I did not know what to make of this new approach. As the singing
got more emotional though, I found myself clapping hands and*

singing out loud just like everyone else.

When the minister finally gave his talk, he told us all about God and Heaven and Salvation. And he said over and over again that all we needed was faith. After his talk we sang some more, and when we finally left the church the minister was standing outside shaking everyone's hand. When my turn came he asked me how I liked the service, and when I told him, he patted me on the shoulder and said I should come back again.

Since I had been given a special invitation by the minister himself, I went to church with Idabel as often as possible. Inside the church I prayed and sang with everyone else, but outside, when I tried to talk to God, I was never really sure anyone was there to listen. Something was missing. And finally one day I found out what it was. Idabel took me one Sunday to a baptism service. My friend, the minister, said, 'unless you are baptized you cannot be pure in heart, and unless you are pure in heart you cannot see God.' 'That's it,' I thought. 'You have to be baptized before you can see God. That's what I've been missing.'

I told Idabel I had to be baptized, and she said we should talk to the minister about it after he was through with the service. He was very nice. He agreed I should be baptized, but he wasn't sure he should do it. When I asked him why, he told me that when a minister baptizes you, you are expected to join his church, and he thought I might be better off if I were baptized in a church that was nearer my home.

I had not realized that joining the church was part of being baptized, and I thought a lot about that at home. I felt one should at least believe in God first before taking a big step like joining a church. When I told Idabel this she said she knew a minister who would baptize me without my having to join his church, and so the next Sunday we went to see what Idabel called an 'Evangelist of the Lord.' He did, indeed, say he would baptize me, but he thought I should ask my parents about it first, especially my father who, being Jewish, might not like the idea too much.

I did not expect any opposition from my mother, who really liked the idea and promised to buy me a pocketbook I had been wanting as a special present. I was more concerned about my father It was hard to figure out how he felt about anything. When I saw him after dinner seated in his chair reading his newspaper, I eased my way into the room, and tried to find a good way to start. I couldn't think of any. So I simply said, 'Father, I've decided to get baptized.'

Father turned his head and looked at me without putting down his paper 'If that's what you want to do,' he said matter-of-factly, 'then by all means do it.'

'You don't mind?' I asked.

'Me? Why should I mind?' he answered.

I still wasn't satisfied. 'Are you sure?'

My father assured me that he was quite certain he did not care. I suppose I should have been pleased; I had gotten what I wanted, and could not understand why I felt so unhappy. Father obviously had nothing more to say, and I left very quickly because I did not want him to notice that I had tears in my eyes. The next day I went back and told the minister that my parents did not object to my being baptized, and so he told me I could be included in the baptism ceremony that was scheduled for the following Sunday. He told me I was to pray in the meantime, and I said I would do the best I could. He told me that was all that was necessary.

Idabel came to my baptism as my witness and my friend. She helped me get ready and put on my white robe. She was very excited, and kept telling me I was going to have the most wonderful experience of my life. I hoped that she was right. After the ceremony I got dressed and went to the minister's study to get my baptismal certificate, while Idabel put my wet things away in a bag we had brought with us. When the minister asked me to spell my last name, I gave him my mother's maiden name. I felt a surge of blood rush to my face, and I couldn't understand what had happened, but I was too embarrassed to correct the mistake. When the minister handed me the certificate, I hid it in my purse, and ran back to Idabel. I never showed the certificate to anyone.

By the time I got home I was feeling quite bleak. Nothing was different. I'd been baptized, but nothing was changed. I still couldn't see God.

I continued going to church regularly with Idabel for a while longer, just in case I hadn't given my baptism time enough to take. And then I went only infrequently, and finally not at all. I told Idabel I simply did not have faith. She said it was probably the work of the devil, and she promised to pray for me. I thanked her for her prayers, and rarely thought of my baptism again. ༄

Having been unable to find the faith she needed in order to find God, Helen decided that the only reality she could now believe in was a rational, logical one. As a result, she decided to become an "intellectual," and began to read omniverously She had plenty of time for this since she had become extremely overweight in her pre-teen years, and the boys in her class didn't seem particularly interested in asking fat girls for dates.

By the time she entered college at New York University, Helen had lost the excess weight, but she had gone through her entire high school career having hardly any social contact with her peers. Consequently she felt particularly awkward in social situations, and seemed to have little to talk about with her academic acquaintances.

Her professors, on the other hand, found her to be an unusually gifted student. They had rarely encountered an undergraduate who had read as extensively or who could discuss as broad a range of academic subjects so intelligently

In college Helen majored in English, which pleased her mother since Helen indicated to the family that she planned on being an English teacher, just like her mother had been prior to her marriage. Helen's real ambition, however—which she kept to herself—was to become a famous author, or more specifically, an internationally famous novelist.

This seemed a strange goal to Helen, for she found writing to be intensely difficult for her Further, she was so sensitive about her writing that even when she finally succeeded in getting something down on paper she was quite likely to hide it and refuse to show it to anyone—including the professor of her creative writing course.

Meanwhile she continued to read a great deal of philosophy as well as literature, and become happily involved in systems of thought, the laws of reasoning, and logic in particular To the business of "living" she paid as little attention as possible.

In her second year at college she met a young man, Louis Schucman, who worked in the college library He was also an "intellectual," and they began talking at length about books and philosophy Louis was only three or four inches taller than the five-foot Helen, and had always felt rather uncomfortable around girls. He was quite delighted to find one who did not make him feel ill-at-ease.

Louis and Helen started to have lunch together every day, and within three months he asked her to marry him. It was the only proposal she had ever received, and it was the only one he had ever made.

22

Helen's mother, although slightly tentative because Louis was Jewish, was nevertheless very enthusiastic about the idea of Helen's marriage. Helen's father, on the other hand, indicated he barely knew the young man and could hardly be expected to have an opinion on the matter

In order to please Louis' parents, Helen and he agreed to have the ceremony in the office of a rabbi. Helen was much too nervous to want anything elaborate, and she asked the rabbi to make the service as short as possible. It was over in less than ten minutes, and afterwards Helen and Louis each went back to their respective homes in order to continue studying for final exams.

Being married had little effect on Helen's life at first. She still had two years of college to finish, and when Louis graduated two weeks after their wedding day, he moved in with Helen and her parents. He did not have enough money to support a wife and an apartment of their own since whatever funds he had accumulated he had invested in a book store which he opened in downtown Manhattan.

The arrangement worked fine as far as Helen was concerned. Her husband was busy with his book business, and she was busy with school. Meals, which Idabel prepared, were always on time, and Helen's father played chess with Louis every evening.

Helen probably would have been delighted to have the situation continue indefinitely, but shortly after her own graduation she and Louis were forced to rent a small apartment of their own when Helen's mother became seriously ill, and the doctor indicated she should give up all housekeeping pressures.

Helen's parents moved to a hotel, and so they no longer had need of Idabel's services. Since she had worked for them for nearly twenty years, though, they felt a real responsibility to her They therefore decided to continue her wages, with her taking care of Helen's new apartment. Helen, who literally did not know how to fry an egg, was extremely grateful for her parents' generosity

After Helen's graduation she tried working in the bookstore, but it became evident after the first week that, for her, being a book seller was particularly unrewarding, distasteful and wearing on her nerves. Nevertheless she continued to go to the store for about a year, when she became very ill and was told by her doctor that she would need an operation. This information frightened her to such an extent that she began having nightmares of being forced down on a table while masks were being held over her face. She resisted the operation for several months until she became so ill she no longer could postpone it. She then talked it over again with the doctor who assured her that the surgery was very simple, and that she would be up and about within a week. Since she was too sick at that point to stall any longer, she arranged to go to the hospital the next day

∽ *That evening I sat down by myself and tried to get organized. It would be much easier, I thought, if I believed God would take care of me. There was a chance, I supposed, that He existed after all. Certainly the fact that I did not believe in Him had nothing to do with His existence one way or another In any case, there could be no harm in attempting a reasonable compromise. I would put the operation in God's hands in case He existed, and if things turned out all right I might even be able to believe in Him again. There was nothing to lose by trying. So I said the Lord's Prayer, put my operation in the hands of God, and went to the hospital the next day with my medal of the Blessed Virgin around my neck.*

As it happened, everything went wrong. I was unconscious for a long time, and did not get out of the hospital for over four months. One of the nurses who took care of me was Catholic and very religious. She thought I was Catholic too, having seen the medal I was wearing. She told me she had been praying for me every day, and had offered up a mass of thanksgiving when I finally regained consciousness. God had been very good to me, she said, and it was a real miracle I had pulled through. I did not see it that way myself. I was very angry about the whole thing, and stayed angry about it for years. If this was God's idea of making things turn out all right, I thought, He certainly had a nasty sense of humor The nurse did not approve of my attitude, and said, rather stiffly, that she would continue to pray for me anyhow. I told the nurse I could not stop her from praying, but added that I would appreciate it if she did not ask God for another miracle until I was at least strong enough to cope with this one. I was, in fact, quite willing to wait a long time before the next one, and I suggested she tell God there was no hurry. What I really needed was to feel better and get out of the hospital, and it did not seem likely to me that prayers would help in this.

Throughout all the long days in the hospital I could hardly wait to get out, but when I finally went home I was not at all enthu-

siastic about it. I felt abandoned by earth as well as Heaven. I was sick for a very long time, but eventually I was forced to recognize that I was better physically and had to declare a moratorium on being an invalid, a decision the doctor felt was long overdue. It was, however, one that left me in a very difficult situation. Being sick had given me something of a vacation from my problems, but the problems were still there, and my being so angry did not help me resolve them.

It finally dawned on me there was a possibility I might have been looking at things the wrong way. Having conceded this much, I began to review my life thus far, and among other things I went over my long and rather erratic search for God. It was clear I had made no progress with that. Admittedly, the fault may have been mine. Perhaps as the nurse had said in the hospital, I did not appreciate all that God had done for me. I had had trouble accepting a miracle once before, as I remembered. Nevertheless, I thought, people can only set up projects as best they can, and in my way I felt I had tried. There was no point in speculating about how the search might have turned out had I undertaken it differently. If God existed, which I very much doubted, He might some day bring up the question of religion Himself. If He did not exist, well, then that's the way it was. For myself, the search was over

I realized, of course, the question of God notwithstanding, that there were other matters that I had too long put off considering. First of all there was the matter of my husband. After all, I was married, and it was about time I got around to think about him. He might be quite nice, I decided. He was not God, of course, but that was probably just as well, all things considered. And he did seem like the sort of person you might work out a reasonably good relationship with. It would take a while, naturally, and might be quite difficult sometimes, but I recognized I might just as well get started on it.

This, I knew, was only one of the steps I had to take, since I also began to realize I needed to find a good way to spend the rest of my life on earth. It was clear to me this might be difficult, since I still knew very little about the world. I did know that being solely a "wife" didn't seem much of an answer for me, especially since Idabel took care of our housekeeping, and we had no children to occupy my time. At first I tried the book business again. My husband, who had spent much of his earlier school years truanting from classes and happily reading in the public library, had collected an excellent library; but to me he still seemed more interested in buying and reading books than in selling them. Nevertheless we managed to struggle by, and finances were not too serious a problem; my father was generally willing to help us out if we really needed anything. But while the book business was clearly the right place for my husband, it was equally clearly the wrong place for me. I began to go there less and less frequently, and usually quarreled with my husband when I did. We just could not seem to get along together in business. I began to feel trapped in a bad situation, without a clear-cut idea of how to get out of it.

For a time it began to look as though my earthly search might end up as ineffectually as my search for Heaven. Yet despite my increasing depression, I had to recognize that I was singularly free to do whatever I wanted. My husband gave me active support and encouragement in planning for an independent career, and my father indicated he would not object to paying whatever expenses might be involved. The problem was that I could not seem to make up my mind about what I wanted to do. It was obvious that I was not going to be the great writer I had once envisioned. However, I continued to consider various other careers largely at the level of fantasy, without seriously considering the necessity of undertaking realistic training. As a matter of fact, by this time I had been out of college for ten years, and was actually quite fearful of going back to school. The truth is that I had become intensely afraid of failure.

My husband showed exemplary patience during our long and frequent discussions about my potential career, but I was so uncertain that it took another ten years before I could arrive at any sort of decision. And even after I had more or less decided to become a psychologist, my efforts were limited for a long time to endless discussions with my husband, writing for course catalogues, and talking about training possibilities with college advisors. Actually, I did not know what psychology was really about, I had only a vague sort of notion that it had some of the answers I needed. I finally made up my mind to overcome my fears and enter graduate school, but at the temporary cost of perspective on the undertaking. I went back to school almost fiercely driven to get top grades. Having failed in the search for Heaven, I was grimly determined to succeed on earth. ✑

Although Helen considered her search for God a closed matter, the subject of religion itself remained far from incidental in her life. As she became more involved in her graduate study program in psychology, she became more and more armed with "facts" and "scientific" weapons which she believed were the final rationale she needed to overcome any last traces of superstition she might have. Thus, she felt she could now look at all things in a highly realistic manner These same facts were also the basis for a subtle but progressive shift that changed her belief system from one of unemotional agnosticism to one of angry atheism. In fact, even before she received her doctoral degree, she was not only ready, but she was *eager* to do battle with anyone who had any thoughts that were even remotely tinged with religious ideas.

Despite—or perhaps because of—her attitude, a series of startling events began to take place in her life. The first one occurred one cold winter evening when she and Louis were taking a long subway ride to visit some friends. Helen detested riding in the subway, and the fact that they had to wait fifteen minutes on the cold platform before a train came by did not help her spirits. When the train finally arrived, it was jammed, and there were no empty seats available. When she and Louis finally did get seats, she was feeling unusually angry and sorry for herself, especially since Louis was buried in his newspaper, completely oblivious to her "suffering." As she looked around the car, all she saw were shabby, dirty looking people. Across the aisle a child with a candy bar pawed at his mother's face, leaving her cheek smudged with chocolate; a child a few seats down picked up some chewing gum from the floor and stuck it in his mouth; and at the far end of the car a group of semi-intoxicated old men were arguing loudly with each other Helen closed her eyes in disgust, feeling sick to her stomach.

And then a stunning thing happened.

A blinding light seemed to blaze up behind her eyes and fill her mind completely Without opening her eyes, she seemed to see a figure, which she knew to be herself, walking directly into the light. The figure seemed to know exactly what she was doing; she paused and knelt down, touching the ground with her elbows, wrists and forehead in what looked like an Eastern expression of deep reverence. Then the figure got up, walked to the side and knelt again, this time resting her head as if leaning against a giant knee.

The outline of a huge arm seemed to reach around her, and then she disappeared. The light grew even brighter, and Helen felt the most indescribably intense love streaming from it. It was so powerful a feeling that she literally gasped and opened her eyes.

She saw the light just an instant longer, during which she loved everyone on the train with that same incredible intensity Then the light faded and the old reality of dirt and ugliness returned to her The contrast was truly shocking, and it took her several minutes to regain a semblance of composure. Then she reached uncertainly for Louis' hand.

"I don't know how to explain this," she said in a shaky voice, "and it's very hard to describe   but, well— " She hesitated a moment, not knowing exactly what to say "Well   .   I saw a great light, and waves and waves of love came out of it, and when I opened my eyes I loved everybody. Then everything disappeared   the feeling, everything. I don't understand what happened."

Louis, who had perused material on mysticism for years, did not seem terribly surprised. "Don't worry about it," he said reassuringly "It's a common mystical experience. Don't give it another thought." And he went back to reading his newspaper

Helen followed his advice, although not with absolute success. Although she did not give any serious thought to it for years, the experience nevertheless remained suspended in a far-off corner of her mind, waiting to be brought into focus again when something of a similar nature might reoccur In the meantime, though, she continued with her studies, her atheism unshaken.

Helen received her doctoral degree in 1957, and was elected to Sigma Xi, the national scientific honorary society Immediately after, a number of opportunities turned up, all of them unsought by her A grant proposal based on her doctoral dissertation was submitted by the university, and was approved for funding. The project turned out well, and the head of the department offered her a teaching assignment. When she submitted additional proposals, however, her luck seemed to change, and when they were turned down, she found herself without a job.

Helen knew that with the excellent connections she had already made, she would have little difficulty in getting an offer for another position. For several weeks, however, she did nothing about it, complaining bitterly to herself about her bad luck, and becoming more and more miserable in the process. Eventually she recognized the unreasonableness of her position, picked up the phone and called one of her friends whom she thought could be of help to her He immediately gave her a list of promising leads. Helen was about to try to reach the first name on the list when the friend called back.

"Forget about the list I gave you," he said emphatically "Do you know Bill Thetford?"

"Never heard of him," she answered.

"Call him right now," the friend continued. "He's Director of the Psychology Program at Presbyterian Hospital. Here's his number And when you get him, be sure to tell him I said he's looking for you."

Helen did not particularly want to work in a medical setting, and the little she had been told about the job was not exactly appealing. Nevertheless, she did pick up the phone, and called Bill Thetford.

The next morning at 10 o'clock when she appeared at the hospital for the interview they had scheduled, she walked into his office, and as she first set eyes on him she made a silent remark which she did not at all understand.

"And there he is," she said to herself; "he's the one I'm supposed to help."

Chapter 3

When Helen arrived at the hospital to begin her job the following
Monday, Bill really didn't know what to do with her Office
space had still not been authorized for the program, and he wasn't
even sure of how the program was to be run

He was, however, able to commandeer a desk for her, and he had
it moved to a free corner in some space adjoining his office That was
to be Helen's headquarters for the next two months

It was not through lack of trying that Bill had been unable to get
approval of additional office space for Helen and other personnel that
were going to be involved He had gone through all kinds of chan-
nels, but he simply could not get anyone—from the Dean on
down—to make a decision

If Bill had known then that the kind of buck-passing he was en-
countering was typical of what he was going to run into in almost
every aspect of his work at the Medical Center, he probably would
have resigned his position immediately. However, he did *not* know
that this kind of behavior was typical, and so he just decided to
bulldog his way through until he got *someone* with the proper
authority to approve at least one of the two plans he had drawn up

One of the main reasons Bill encountered so many frustrating
problems was that he was responsible to five different specific
officials—The Chairman of the Psychiatry Department, the President of the hospital, the Vice-President in charge of Professional Af-
fairs, the Dean of the College of Physicians and Surgeons and the
President of Columbia University—as well as to various other vice-
presidents of special services As a result, it was almost impossible
to get anything done, much less get anything done in an expeditious
manner And yet one of his jobs was to initiate changes in order to

work out many of the problems that had been multiplying over the years Every step of the way—no matter what he was trying to accomplish—he met massive resistance from medical professionals and administrative personnel who were constantly striving to protect and enlarge their own domains

In addition, the Psychology Department, a division of the Department of Psychiatry, ranked about as close to the bottom of the priority list as any department in the hospital There had been very little active interest in the department before Bill arrived, and salaries for the professional staff were lower than those for secretaries. Although Bill felt it important to replace various staff people who were unqualified, it was virtually impossible to find qualified people who would replace them at the salary level the hospital offered

These were just some of the problems Bill was faced with when Helen joined the department, and it did not take her long to draw an accurate picture of the situation Two months went by before office space was finally assigned to the project, and by that time Helen, still working from the "temporary" corner Bill had found for her the first day, was on the verge of resigning In view of later events, however, it seems that choice was not really hers to make; this was where she was *supposed* to remain

Even in her new quarters, however, Helen found the job ghastly at first Not only was she now located in a different building than Bill, with whom she was working very closely, but the work was the dullest, and the situation the most difficult of her life Besides the work being routine, Helen sensed rather quickly an atmosphere of suspicion and competitiveness to which she had previously not been exposed

What's more, Helen and Bill faced another, more serious problem Although each had tremendous respect for the other's abilities, more often than not each also seemed to bring out the worst in the other's personality This became apparent within a few months, and added greatly to the tension in each one's life For it seemed that whether they were working on a grant proposal together, or merely deciding whether to eat lunch at the hospital or in a small restaurant, there was no way for them to reach easy agreements

Despite this, or perhaps because of it, they each basically knew they needed the other's support and sustenance in order to cope

31

with the multitude of problems they jointly faced in their professional environment. For it was obvious to them both that they *had* to do something to try to change the feelings of hostility and resentment that seemed to be instilled in so many of the people with whom they had to deal; without the hope of such change, it was clear that each would have looked for another—more peaceful—place to work.

And so they agreed to try to work out the departmental problems together At first their attempts were heart-breaking. Their initial efforts were spent in frantically writing up grant proposals against deadlines in attempts to bring in funds that were urgently needed in so many of the department's areas of responsibility. And though there was no question that they had a common goal, it appeared that Bill could not write a paragraph that Helen wouldn't rigorously edit, while Helen couldn't make a suggestion that Bill wouldn't intensely question.

The work itself was exhausting, and their conflictual attitudes made it doubly so. They worked evenings and week-ends, and argued on the phone from home when they weren't together And as time went on it seemed that all their efforts produced very little progress. Political divisiveness continued, and interpersonal relations seemed to get no better Staff turnover was enormous, putting even more pressure on Bill to try to keep things running at least at a level that was no worse than usual.

Despite their almost single-minded efforts to work toward a common goal, their personal relationship reflected the stress they were experiencing. They were an unlikely team to begin with. Bill, who was fourteen years younger than Helen, was an inherent optimist who, despite the formidable obstacles he faced, maintained a persistent underlying belief that there was a real way out of any difficult situation, and with perseverence one could always find it. Helen, on the other hand, was anxious to the point of agitation, and though she tried to maintain a facade of cheerfulness, her underlying pessimism and insecurity always showed through. Besides, they handled their interpersonal problems in very different ways. Bill was more apt to withdraw when he perceived a situation as becoming demanding or coercive, while Helen tended to become overly-involved, with a resulting consequence of feeling trapped, resentful and imposed upon. Thus, while their interdependence had grown, they had also

32

developed even more anger towards each other since neither could change the other's attitude, and their genuine attempts to cooperate were hampered by their growing resentments.

Despite personal feelings such as these, there was a sense of shared commitment between them that kept Helen from resigning, and that impelled Bill to "protect" Helen's future. When the original grant, under which Helen had been hired, was downgraded and the project was destined to be curtailed, Bill appointed Helen to the only staff vacancy that was under his direct control, thus insuring her of at least some sort of job security

In 1963 the chairman of the department appointed Bill to the Research Planning Committee, a group whose responsibility was the allocation of space in the new research building that was about to be constructed. This was a singular honor for Bill—one he had not been offered before, and one he was never offered again. Having the opportunity, for the first time, to actually create office space for his own use, Bill had plans drawn up for two private offices and a secretarial area in a remote section of the building, away from the ordinary flow of traffic. He did not know at the time why he arranged for two private offices since he had no reason to. As he said years later, "I had absolutely no inkling of how necessary it was for me and Helen to be together "

In the summer of 1965, the new research building was completed and ready for occupancy In the midst of their professional and personal struggle Bill arranged to move into the new building and suggested that Helen occupy the second private office adjacent to his. Although their psychological difficulties continued, the physical obstacles to their collaborative work had been eliminated.

One afternoon that summer before a weekly research meeting which neither of them looked forward to attending because of the savage competition which usually surfaced during these sessions, something happened. Bill went into Helen's office and obviously wanted to say something which he evidently found hard to talk about. At last he took a deep breath, grew slightly red-faced and delivered a speech. He admitted later that the words sounded trite and sentimental, and he hardly expected a favorable response from Helen. Nevertheless, he said what he felt he had to say He had been thinking things over and had concluded that their approach was

33

wrong. "There must," he said, "be another way Our attitudes are so negative that we can't work anything out." He went on to say that he had therefore decided to try to look at things differently

He proposed, quite specifically, to try out the new approach that day at the research meeting. He was not going to get angry, and he was determined to look for a constructive side in what the people there said and did. He was going to cooperate rather than compete. He said they had obviously been headed the wrong way and it was time to find a new direction. It was a long speech for Bill, and he spoke with unaccustomed emphasis. Then he waited in some discomfort for Helen's response. It was not the one he expected. She jumped up, told Bill with conviction that he was right, and said she would join in the new approach with him.

At some level this joining represented a *real* commitment that was unprecedented in their relationship, and it seemed to be the signal for the beginning of a series of remarkable events that occurred during the summer of 1965.

The staff meeting at which Bill began his new approach to problem solving began no differently than dozens of similar meetings they had attended over the years, but as various views and positions were defended and others were attacked, some of the participants sensed a subtle difference in the overall atmosphere in the room. Where Bill had previously defended, he now simply listened and agreed to consider When staff members made excuses for work not completed, their excuses were accepted with the added hope that the next time the individual in question might not be as burdened with extra work. Surprisingly to Bill, his responses seemed to generate similar responses in others at the meeting.

Although no major breakthroughs in relationships were accomplished during the first weeks of their search for a "better way," Bill and Helen did agree that they noticed a distinctly less aggressive atmosphere at the meetings they were attending, and by the end of the summer the interpersonal climate within the whole department had almost completely changed. Tensions lessened. Antagonisms dropped away Many of the under-qualified staff members left the department (on friendly terms) while much more competent people showed up to replace them almost immediately Bill's and Helen's efforts were not always consistent, and were even sometimes half-hearted, but the underlying commitment remained strong, and there was no doubt that their efforts helped to bring about some remarkable results. Within three months the department showed signs of functioning in a smoother way, while morale began to improve to the point where Bill noticed that staff members actually smiled at each other from time to time.

Their initial efforts at healing their own relationship were not as successful, however Although they tried to be charitable and understanding, somehow the psychological obstacles they faced were often too steep for them to overcome. Thus, while relationships with those in the department—and in other departments—continued to improve dramatically, they themselves still experienced outbreaks of extreme antagonism toward each other And though the basis for their discord would later be recognized as trivial or even non-existent, they still knew very clearly that they had a tremendous amount of serious work to do if they were to overcome the almost Pavlovian responses to which they had become accustomed.

It was while they were assiduously trying to straighten things out between themselves that Helen began to experience a change in her "mental pictures"—those images she had been seeing on and off for as long as she could remember The black and white "still shots" which she often saw were suddenly beginning to appear to her not only in color, but also in full motion, and in meaningful sequences as well. Her dreams began to take on the same characteristics, and they often continued a theme that had begun before she fell asleep.

∽ *Between June, when Bill and I made our joint commitment to change our attitudes, and October, three more or less distinct sequential lines of fantasy and dreams reached my startled awareness. Although they overlapped one another to some extent, I will describe them separately in order to impart whatever clarity I can hope for I have no idea if they were symbolic representations, much like dream imagery, or if they were somehow related to actual events. I watched them as if I were looking at a motion picture, and felt myself more as an audience than a participator even while I was looking at a figure which I knew to be myself.*

The first of the three series was introduced by a picture of an unrecognized female figure, heavily draped and kneeling with bowed head, heavy chains twisted around her wrists and ankles. Next to her a fire rose high above her head, coming from a large metal brazier standing near her on a low tripod. She seemed to be some sort of priestess, and the fire appeared to be associated with an ancient religious rite. This figure recurred almost daily for several weeks, though each time with noticeable changes. The chains began to drop away and she began to raise her head. Very slowly she finally stood up, with only a short, unconnected length of chain still tied to her left wrist. The fire blazed with unaccustomed brightness as she rose. I was quite unprepared for the intensity of my emotional reactions to her, and did not understand them at all.

When the priestess figure first raised her eyes and looked at me I was terribly afraid. I was sure her expression would be full of anger and her eyes filled with condemnation and disdain. I kept my head turned away the next few times she appeared, but finally I made up my mind to look straight at her face. When I did I burst into tears. Her face was gentle and full of compassion, and her eyes were beyond description. The best word I could find in describing her to Bill was 'innocent.' She had never seen what I was afraid she would find in me. She knew of nothing that warranted condemnation. I loved her so much that I literally fell on my knees in front of her Then I tried unsuccessfully to unite with her as she stood facing me, either by slipping over to her side or drawing her to mine.

My next reactions were even stranger. I was suddenly swept away by a sense of joy so intense I could hardly breathe. Aloud I asked, 'Does this mean I can have my function back?' The answer, silent but perfectly clear, was, 'Of course!' I would not have believed it was possible to experience such happiness as that answer called forth in me, and for a little while I kept repeating, 'How wonderful! Oh, how wonderful!' There seemed to be no doubt that there was a part of me I did not know, but which understood exactly what all this really meant. It was a strangely split awareness, of a kind I was to become much more familiar with later

The second series of pictures, which like the first reached me sometimes in short glimpses rather like daydreams and sometimes in sleeping dreams, included Bill as well as myself. We turned up in various relationships, but the actual chronology was quite confused. Situations which seemed to be very old often came after almost contemporary ones. In the first picture of this series

I saw myself in a boat, rowing frantically but not getting anywhere. Looking about, I identified the place as Venice and the boat as a gondola. Nearby was a tall thin man, quite reminiscent of Bill, leaning against a striped wooden post protruding from the water His arms were folded across his chest, and he was watching me with mock seriousness. I grew more and more sure it was Bill, dressed as a gondolier but with gleaming sequins scattered across the costume. He neither moved nor spoke. Then I noticed that the gondola was tied to a wharf with a heavy rope. It was a silly situation; I had been working hard at the impossible. Bill did not offer help, but his smile was not unkind.

The next few events in this series had different feelings to them. Bill showed up once as a bullfighter in a spectacular costume, gold from head to foot. There was a dim impression of an arena in the background, but that was most unclear His next appearance was a witch doctor, with feathers around his ankles and wrists and dressed in a straw skirt and an imposing headdress of bright feathers and gleaming jewels. I wore a simple homespun dress. We were both black, and were in a clearing in a thick jungle. I seemed to have come to Bill for help, and he was responding to my appeal with a weird dance, accompanied by loud cries in a language I did not understand. At first I felt comforted. Then I became afraid and begged him to stop. He did not seem to hear me through the sound of the banging of crude wooden instruments he was holding and the increasingly loud beating of drums in the backbround. I crept away terrified, holding my hands over my ears in a frantic effort to shut out the sounds. I did not look back.

The next episode involving Bill and myself seemed like a story within a story. One theme in various phases extended for quite a while before reaching its grim conclusion. I was a priestess in what looked like an Egyptian temple, although I have an idea that it might have been even older Huge stone statues were vaguely outlined along the sides and back of the building, but I could not make them out clearly because the interior was so dimly lit. Even in the half light, however, I could tell that the temple was very large and extremely imposing. The altar, the only brightly-lighted part of the building, was particularly splendid. A blazing light shone down on it from a source I could not identify. Magnificent jewels glowed all around it, and its smooth, polished stone surfaces reflected the light like mirrors. As the high priestess I was very elaborately dressed, and wearing a heavily inlaid crown from

37

which the large center stone was missing.

In the opening episode of the series I was standing at the altar leaning over Bill who was lying on the floor almost naked. The shaft of a spear was in my hands, with the point resting on Bill's forehead between his eyes. Then came an extended series of flashbacks of what had led up to this opening scene. There had been a slave uprising. I was about to kill Bill, the leader of the revolt, who had managed to steal the large center ruby from the priestess' crown. It was not an ordinary ruby. It gave its wearer magical powers. The thief had to be killed if these powers were to return to the priestess, whose religion was power and enslavement. To revolt against her was to ask for death.

What happened next was entirely out of character I was aware of feelings of intense rage and vindictiveness as I prepared to force the point of the spear between Bill's eyes. He did not seem particularly frightened. He merely looked up at me and waited. I braced myself, ready to bring the spear down. Entirely unexpectedly I hesitated just an instant, and knew it was all over with me. Bill would live and I would die. As I threw the spear down my death was certain. The final episode in the series found me standing alone on the top step of a wide stairway before an enormous bolted door I was outside the temple. My crown and my golden gown were gone. I was wearing a loose white dress, smudged at the sides and torn at the neck. Before me was nothing but desert. The wind blew hot sand against my face, and I could see whitened bones scattered about in the distance. Mine would soon be among them. I cursed myself bitterly for allowing this to happen. Anger literally shook me as I walked slowly down the stairway, with thirst already biting at my throat and the smell of death in the wind.

The emotional effect of this last episode was intense and long-lasting. I still felt the anger after the images faded, and it later blazed into open fury as I told Bill the story the next day, particularly when I spoke of the theft of the ruby. It was as if it were happening all over again. A picture of the ruby, beautiful and blazing red, rose before my eyes, and for a brief period the scene became reality for me. Again I berated myself for dying for a rebellious slave who was nothing but a common thief. I could barely contain my fury at Bill, who was understandably upset. So was I. The intensity of my anger was quite surprising to both of us. It was a while before the next episodes in the series appeared. It was almost as though I had to recover a little before going on. For-

tunately, the next installment was different, although it too, did not turn out too well for me.

Bill, a Franciscan monk dressed in a brown robe and sandals, was silently reading from a small book as he walked up and down an arched monastery corridor bordering on a small, well-kept green lawn. There was a lovely fountain in the middle, with birds bathing in the basin and rows of bright flowers around its base and scattered in patches over the grass. The time was uncertain, but the monastery seemed to be in Spain. I was walking slowly down the corridor toward Bill, dressed all in black. My face was heavily veiled, my eyes were cast down, and my hands were clasped as if in prayer When I reached Bill I knelt as a penitent, and humbly asked him for forgiveness. He did not look up. Anger took hold of me, and I rose and accused him of being heartless. He did not seem to hear me, merely continuing serenely to read. His eyes never moved from the book. I backed away in anger and helpless frustration. The picture faded out slowly and inconclusively.

The next scene, in order of appearance, seemed so ancient that it appeared to be taking place at the very beginning of time. I was a priestess again, but this time of a very different kind. This priestess was, in fact, much like the one with the innocent eyes I had watched emerging from heavy chains into freedom. She was hidden from the world in a small white marble temple set in a broad and very green valley. I was not sure that her body was entirely solid. Actually what was seen was little more than an outline of a small, slender woman dressed in white, who never came further into the world than the doorway of the little room which contained a plain wooden altar A small flame burned on it, sending up a steady column of white smoke. The priestess stayed close to the altar, sitting on a low wooden stool and praying with closed eyes for those who came to her for help.

Sometimes I saw only the valley outside the temple. At times there seemed to be no one there, but at other times there was a huge column of people marching together very joyously. The column seemed to extend endlessly in both directions, and I could somehow feel the deep sense of freedom and unity each individual was experiencing as he marched ahead to certain victory. I was not sure what the exact role of the priestess was in helping them all, but I was somehow convinced that her prayers made a vital contribution. I was also sure that people came to her for help from all over; some in fact from very far away. They did not, however, speak to her directly. They knelt on the ledge that ran around a low wall which separated the inner and outer parts of the temple, and stated their needs to a man who seemed to be serving as a sort of intermediary between the priestess and the world. He remained in a large, enclosed space that separated the priestess from those who came for help. The man conveyed their needs to her

I did not see the man's face for some time, and it took me even longer to recognize him as Bill. He played a crucial role in enabling the priestess to fulfill her function. When people told him what they needed, he went to the door of her room and merely told her that there had been a request for help. He said only that a brother had come for healing, and then he asked for help on behalf of the brother The priestess never asked for anyone's name, nor the details of his request. She prayed for everyone in the same way, sitting very quietly beside the flame on the altar It never occured to her that help would not be granted. She never really left God's side, and she remained peacefully certain of His presence there in the room with her I was sure she was myself, and yet I was not sure. What was certain was that I watched her with great love.

The next episode was again a dramatic contrast. Bill and I were now both slaves in what seemed to be mid-19th century America. We were married, but I was quite contemptuous of him. He was older than I, much darker in skin coloring, and very religious in what seemed to me to be a very simple-minded way. I saw no justification for the childlike trust he had in God. He had a similarly naive trust in me, and for this I knew there was no reason. The actual story is vague, but I gathered that certain definite things were happening. I was beautiful, almost white in appearance, and completely amoral. White men took a liking to me, and I traded favors readily enough. Somehow I made a deal whereby I gained my liberty, but in some way at Bill's expense. I did not hide my plans from him. In fact, I took pleasure in telling him all about them. He did not condemn me, nor make an attempt to interfere. I turned my back on him and flounced out. But I remembered the sadness in his eyes.

The series ended on a note of final achievement and even glory. I was standing in a room that seemed to be on the top floor of a church building. Bill, seated at a large, old-fashioned church organ, was playing Handel's Hallelujah Chorus, his face lit with joy. We had finally reached our goal. I was standing in front of a simple brown wooden altar, on which two words were written one underneath the other I cannot imagine a less appropriate word pair The top word was 'Elohim,' which I did not recognize at the time, and only later discovered is one of the Hebrew names for God. The other word 'Evoe' I did identify as the cry of the Greek Bacchantes in celebrating the rites of Bacchus. As I watched, a streak of lightning from the back of the church struck the altar and obliterated the second word entirely. Only 'Elohim' remained, written in bright gold letters. The Hallelujah Chorus rose to a crescendo, and a figure outlined in brilliant light which I recognized immediately as Jesus stepped from behind the altar and came toward me. I started to kneel in front of him, but he came around to my side and knelt at the altar with me. Bill rose and knelt at his other side. And then a Voice, with which I was to become increasingly familiar, said in silent but perfectly clear words, 'That altar is within you.' The emotional impact of the conclusion was so powerful that I burst into tears.

The third series of pictures, which occurred to me the same way as the others, lasted longer and fell into a definite progression. Throughout this series a male figure of uncertain identity turned up apparently to help out from time to time. Generally I did not recognize him at all. At times I thought he might be Bill. At other times I vaguely suspected he might be Jesus. This series began much as had the previous one, and at a somewhat less obvious level as the first one had as well. Wandering along the shore of a lake, I came upon a deserted boat laying on its side. It was held down by thick ropes attached to a heavy anchor sunk deep into the mud that also covered part of the boat itself. The boat had obviously been abandoned years ago.

I knew I could not possibly release the boat without help, but I nevertheless felt impelled to try. I tugged futilely at the ropes, which were so heavy I could barely lift them. Besides, the mud was slippery and I kept falling. I called out for help but there was no one within earshot. The place was utterly deserted. It was a frustrating situation. I somehow realized the importance of freeing the boat, but I was also aware of my complete inability to do so. And then the answer came to me. I had been going about it wrong.

'Of course,' I said to myself. 'Inside the boat is a very powerful receiving and sending set. It hasn't been used for a long time, but it still works. And that's the only way I'll get help.'

At this point the first episode was over

Several unclear things happened next. A man turned up from

41

somewhere, and together we managed to drag the anchor out of the mud, set the boat up straight and finally get it into the water. Then it began to move, though the anchor still dragged a little at first. The boat gained momentum after a while, however, and seemed to be embarking on a very definite course. I had no idea where it was going, but apparently I did not need to know. It seems that the man, who I noticed suddenly was with me, did know. And that was sufficient.

After the boat had gone a way the water got choppy, and I was beginning to get afraid. Fortunately, the man turned up in the next episode dressed for the occasion: in a yellow slicker, helmet and boots. I was steering uncertainly when he arrived. He took the wheel from me.

'You go over there and sit down,' he said in a firm but not unfriendly tone. 'It's going to be heavy weather for a while. I'll get you through this, and then you can steer again.'

I sat down on a bench on the side of the deck, but I was still a little uneasy.

'Maybe we should call for more help,' I suggested, timidly. 'I think there's a very good receiving and sending set inside this boat. Maybe we could use that.'

'You just keep away from that now,' said the man, quickly and still more firmly. 'You're not ready. You'd merely get into trouble. When you're ready to use it I'll tell you. Meanwhile don't worry. We'll make it.'

I watched, reassured, as he very adroitly brought the boat through a very narrow passage with a storm raging all around us. Big waves rose over the prow of the boat, and rain poured down from a black sky. Oddly enough, I did not even get wet. Gradually the boat emerged into quiet waters and I found the steering wheel again in my own hands.

The man turned up next lounging against the side of the boat, comfortably dressed in shorts and an open-necked summer shirt. The weather was warm and sunny, the water smooth and the boat easy to steer We were standing at the wheel and chatting. I noticed he wore a gold chain around his neck, with an unfamiliar gold symbol hanging from it. I thought it might perhaps be a Hebrew letter Then I remembered something.

'I have one like that,' I said, looking at the symbol. 'In fact, I'm wearing it right now.'

'Indeed I know that,' replied the man, smiling.

42

'The only thing is,' I added, 'Mine goes the other way.'

'I know that, too,' said the man, still smiling. 'As a matter of fact this one happens to be yours, too. I'll keep it for you a while longer, but I promise to give it to you when you can use it.'

The two symbols, mirror images of each other, remained so clearly in my mind that I copied them down afterwards. Some time later I ran across a friend who was a Hebrew scholar, and I asked him if he recognized them. He was puzzled at first, and then said, 'Of course! The symbol of the miracle of the reversal.' He had to explain to me what he meant. When Moses came down from the mountain where he had talked with God, he carried a scroll on which God's words were written. The miracle was that the words could be read correctly from either side of the scroll, which was obviously not possible by ordinary means. My reactions to this information were curiously mixed. On the one hand I was delighted and also impressed. On the other hand I was afraid. I still found it difficult to believe that dreams and fantasies were more than unrealistic attempts at wish-fulfillment, and I was therefore able to dismiss much of what I had already seen and heard. This, however, was difficult to pass by quite so casually. ✍

Helen reported these experiences, as they occurred, both to Bill and her husband. Louis, like Helen, seemed to find the overall situation very anxiety provoking, and so she simply ceased telling him what was happening to her. Bill, on the other hand, was extremely interested in the series of images. This did not help lessen Helen's anxieties, however, and even though Bill was totally supportive of her, she still felt terribly threatened by the phenomena. She didn't like them, she didn't want them, and in general they made her feel particularly anxious, for she believed the kind of imagery she was involved in was the kind she might expect to hear about from psychiatric patients who came to see her

As her experiences continued, she even told Bill she felt she might be going crazy, and that she really should submit to a psychiatric examination.

"Why don't you just let it be, and go along with it. I have a feeling it may have something to do with that speech I made to you about finding a better way of dealing with difficult relationships," he added reassuringly.

43

Although Bill, like Helen, had had no interest in—or knowledge of—anything remotely concerned with psychic phenomena, it was obvious to him that something paranormal was certainly going on here, and he found the material itself absolutely fascinating. On the other hand, one of the things that bothered Helen most was the thought that the whole situation might indeed *have* something to do with the psychic—a thought that was particularly fear provoking to her, even though she knew absolutely nothing about anything "psychic" except that the world-renowned psychologist, Dr J.B. Rhine, had done some experiments with cards at Duke University in North Carolina.

Because of his inquiring nature, and in order to arm himself with as much information as possible so as to better understand what was happening, Bill began to search out books about psychic phenomena. One of the first he read was about the life of Edgar Cayce. Cayce, sometimes referred to as "America's greatest psychic," had died in 1945 after having lived through almost forty years of rationally unexplainable experiences, almost all of which had been transcribed at the time they occurred, and which could therefore be studied at the library of the Association for Research and Enlightenment (A.R.E.) in Virginia Beach, an organization founded to perpetuate Cayce's insights.

When Bill told Helen a little bit about Cayce, and suggested she might find it interesting to read the book he had found, she flatly declined to look at it. She refused to admit there was even anything discussable about her experiences, although she had to admit to Bill that her attitude did have a certain inconsistency to it. On the one hand she knew that the incident involving the "reversal miracle" was something she had no intellectual, conscious knowledge of, and yet she refused to offer any suggestion as to how the information could have come to her

Bill was not in the least put off by Helen's attitude, and he became increasingly interested in some of the parapsychological literature, for somewhere deep inside himself he knew that what Helen was going through was extremely important for the two of them.

When Bill suggested to Helen that many of the images she had described suggested to him that past lives might somehow be involved, Helen became particularly upset. First of all, she couldn't

44

understand how Bill, who she knew had never had any belief whatsoever in reincarnation, could seriously suggest such a thing. And, second, with her highly "intellectual" background, and with the great emphasis she gave to "scientific proof," the mere suggestion of such a concept brought forth from her icily derisive reactions. However, as her imaging experiences continued, her attitude did begin to show a slight change.

ꙮ When the next episode took place it arrived in the form of a dream. In usual dream fashion, the boat had turned into a car I was crossing a bridge in very heavy traffic. I wanted to make a right turn, but I was in the wrong lane and another car was blocking my way. Both of us were crowded in, with cars in front and behind. The whole situation seemed to be one large traffic jam. There seemed to be no way I could make the turn, even though it was essential that I do so. 'If I try to turn I'll crash into that car next to me,' I thought, 'and if he turns right I won't have time to follow before the gap will close and I'll be jammed in again.' I kept trying to think up ways to make the turn, but all of them were inadequate and some disastrous. And then the solution came to me.

'We'll both make it together,' I thought, happily. 'It won't be any trouble at all.'

And so I made the turn along with the man in the car next to me. It was very easy. 'It's funny I never thought of that before,' I said to myself as the picture faded.

Next time I found myself back in the boat, still aware of having taken a right turn. The boat was moving slowly but easily along a very straight little canal. There was just enough breeze to help the boat along. The sides of the canal were lined with lovely old trees and green lawns edged with banks of flowers. 'I wonder if there's buried treasure here,' I thought to myself, dreamily. 'I shouldn't be surprised if there were.' Then I noticed a long pole with a large hook on the end, lying on the bottom of the boat. 'Just the thing,' I thought, dropping the hook into the water, and reaching the pole down as far as I could. The hook caught something heavy, and I raised it with difficulty. It was an ancient treasure chest, the wood worn from the water and the bottom covered with seaweed. I managed to get it into the boat and opened it excitedly.

I was bitterly disappointed. I had expected jewels or coins, but there was nothing in the chest but a large black book. The binding was like the 'spring binders' used for temporarily holding manuscripts or papers together On the spine one word was written in gold. The word was 'Aesculapius.' The word was familiar but I could not remember what it meant. When I looked it up, I found it was the name of the Greek god of healing. I saw the same book two more times during the next week. Once there was a string of pearls around it; the other time was in a dream in which I saw a stork flying over some villages, and wondered what was so important about that. It was then that a silent Voice said to me, 'Look at what the stork is carrying.' I did. In the pouch was not the expected baby, but the same kind of black book; the only difference was that this one had a gold cross on the cover The Voice then said, 'This is your book.' Neither Bill nor I had any idea what the book stood for until much later

Although the idea of reincarnation was particularly repugnant to me, it was clear to me that many of the images I was having seemed to be flashbacks of myself at various times and in different places. I explained these experiences to Bill as being the usual dream symbolism with which any clinical psychologist is familiar I admit, however, that as the images continued, my dogmatism on the subject did show some slight—very slight—signs of abating.

I watched these flashback pictures as a spectator, though with little doubt the figures represented myself. In one of the earlier scenes I saw a thin, frail girl in an opulent French drawing-room. The time seemed to be around the middle of the 18th Century. The girl, dressed in white, was playing a musical instrument resembling a harpsichord in a gathering of magnificently dressed ladies and gentlemen, apparently guests at a lavish social event. The girl was eighteen at most, and obviously ill. 'She's too fragile,' I said to myself. 'She won't live another year She can't do anything but just fade away. It's a mistake. She's never going to make it.' A splendidly dressed butler stepped out and closed the drawing room door The girl disappeared. Shortly afterwards there was a very vague picture of a girl, slightly older than the first, lying on the straw-covered floor of an airless room in a prison. Her arms were bound tightly together and her feet were chained to the floor The time seemed to be somewhere around the 12th or 13th century, and I had an idea that the girl was executed in the end.

Several subsequent pictures showed the image of a nun, apparently in different countries and at various dates. The clearest of these pictures was of an elderly, arthritic, and disappointed *nun, worn thin and ill by a life of severe austerities, and emotionally warped and sterile. She was walking down the side aisle of a very large and beautiful church, strikingly reminiscent of the Cathedral of Notre Dame in Paris. The aisle was dim, and the candle the nun held helped only a little. As she walked she ran her hand along the grey stone wall beside her, as if searching for a door or perhaps more literally a way out. She did not find it. The grim lines on her face deepened as I watched. 'She does not know,' I thought. 'She's trying, but she does not know.' I was repelled by her harsh expression, but I felt a deep sympathy for her lost cause.*

In striking contrast to that grim figure was another which recurred at intervals and still crosses my mind every once in a while. This one was the only image that kept returning in completely unchanged form. It was a picture of a young girl who resembled me in many ways, although she could not have been more than sixteen years old at most. Her head was slightly thrown back in happy laughter, and her arms were outstretched as if in universal welcome. She seemed to be wholly joyous; literally incapable of experiencing grief or pain. She was standing on a lawn of bright young grass, but in her extraordinary happiness her bare feet hardly seemed to touch the ground at all. She was dressed in a light, loose dress which was not reminiscent of any particular time or place. There was, in fact, nothing suggesting the past about her, nor did she seem likely to be concerned about the future. I do not think she even regarded time as we do. ✍

As Bill's reading of parapsychological literature continued, he became more and more interested in the Cayce material. What he considered both impressive and important in these accounts was the evidence which suggested that minds can communicate with each other by some paranormal means as yet unknown to science, and he frequently discussed this with Helen. Because Helen respected his opinion—even though she thought he was way off on this one—she did, finally, ask him for a book on the subject and he chose for her a biography of Cayce written by his son, Hugh Lynn. There was little doubt that Helen found it interesting although she was still repelled by what she regarded as its "spooky" and more incredible aspects. When Bill suggested that she had had some rather unusual experiences herself recently she conceded that this was true, and, indeed, further events were to take place shortly thereafter which

Helen would be hard put to explain.

⟲The new phase began one day when Bill and I were concentrating on a research report. Suddenly I laid the papers down, and said, with great urgency, 'Quick, Bill! Your friend Alan, the one we met in Chicago a while back, he's thinking about suicide. We must send him a message.' Bill sat down next to me, as I sent an earnest mental message to Alan asking him to reconsider. Afterwards, I said to Bill, 'I'll bet there was nothing to it.' I was wrong, however; it turned out that I had been quite accurate. It was hard not to be impressed, particularly as surprising events continued to happen. Bill went to an out-of-town meeting, and on his return I described the place where he had stayed in great detail even though I had never seen it. I also told him about some of the things that had happened there before he had a chance to tell me about them. I also gave him a very detailed description of a friend's house where he stayed for a week-end, even to the colors of the walls and furniture. Later, when he went on vacation quite far away, I sent him a mental image of a gold pin he should bring me. He handed me the pin on his return. There was little doubt that it was the one I had asked for.

My reactions to episodes of this kind were curiously mixed. I was actually becoming rather proud of the acquisition of such dramatic abilities, and I even caught brief glimpses of fantasies of power and prestige crossing the back of my mind. At the same time, I went to great lengths to explain the episodes away because they aroused considerable fear. For a while, the idea of psychic powers gained simultaneously in attraction and fear for me, and I began to have nightmares the content of which I could not remember. As the list of surprising events grew, I could not get over a sense of evil and even witchcraft that I somehow associated with them. Yet pride kept pace with anxiety, and though I felt an increasing sense of danger I also experienced a concomitant feeling of self-inflation.

While I was still in the 'magic' phase, an event took place which involved a strange mixture of fact and fantasy, and which also seemed to point to a definite future direction. The episode included a number of levels, beginning with evident magical overtones, continuing to more apparent religious imagery, and concluding on a simple, real-life note. The hospital wanted to send Bill and myself to the Mayo Clinic to study their evaluation procedures. The evening before we left, a picture crossed my mind that was so sharp I felt impelled to describe it in writing. It was a picture of a church, the details of which stood out with startling clarity. I was uncertain of its denomination at first, but finally settled on Lutheran. I seemed to be looking down on it from above, at an angle at which I might be seeing it from a low-flying plane. The picture was so sharp that I abandoned caution entirely, and told Bill I was sure we would see the building when we landed in Minnesota the next day.

I was disappointed and angry when we saw nothing of the sort. In an attempt to restore my self-esteem, I said I was sure we would find that church somewhere in the town. It was late when we arrived, we were tired, but he understood. He suggested that we take a cab after dinner and try to find my church. I picked out several names from the church directory, but they did not turn out to be right. Then I described my church to the driver, and asked him if he knew of one reasonably like it. He did not sound hopeful, although we tried a few more at his suggestion. At length Bill wisely suggested that we forget the whole thing. It was getting very late. Back at the hotel, Bill spoke to me very firmly.

'Your church isn't here,' he said, 'and you're acting very strangely about it. What's all this desperation about? Go to sleep and forget it, and I'll see you in the morning.'

When I met Bill the next morning we were both red-eyed and tired. We had barely slept. We got through our tightly scheduled day somehow, and toward evening drove wearily out to the airport. Bill went to look at a newsstand while I sat down and closed my eyes. I was too tired to look at anything. I was just dozing off . . .

'And here's your church,' said Bill, holding a picture in a guidebook in front of me.

'Oh, yes, that's it!' I said, eagerly. 'Where is it?'

'Nowhere,' answered Bill. 'Here. Read about it yourself.'

The church was indeed nowhere now. It had once occupied the site of the Mayo Clinic, but was torn down when the hospital was built.

'So that's why I was looking down on it when I saw it,' I told Bill. 'It was because it's in the past. It had nothing to do with airplanes.'

And then a chill went over me and I did not want to talk about the church any more.

We had to change planes late that night on the way home, and waited almost an hour in a cold almost-deserted airport. Huddled against a wall was a young woman obviously traveling by herself. I could feel waves and waves of misery going through her I mentioned her to Bill, who indicated he was against my talking to her We were both exhausted, and he did not feel up to getting involved with strangers at that point. Besides, he said I might well be simply imagining her distress since she did not give any outward signs of anything but sleepiness. I could not, however, escape from the strong feelings of pain I was receiving from her Finally I told Bill I could not help myself, and went to talk to her

Her name was Charlotte, and she said she was scared stiff. She had never flown before. Would I sit with her and hold her hand? I took her over to Bill, and suggested that we put her in between us so she would have a friend on both sides. Bill was courteous but unhappy. It had been a difficult trip and he would have preferred a peaceful trip home. Charlotte shook as the plane took off, but I held her hand and she calmed down quickly. She wanted to talk. It seemed she had found her life 'closing in' on her, and so she had summarily left her husband and three children, and headed for the only place she could think of – New York City. She had done remarkably little planning, having taken only a small suitcase of personal clothing, and having no idea where she would stay once she got to New York. She was, however, not worried. She had several hundred dollars with her She was a Lutheran, and she was sure all she had to do was find a Lutheran church in New York and they would take care of her there. Bill and I exchanged glances. The message was not hard to grasp. 'And this,' I seemed to hear, 'is my true church   helping another; not the edifice you saw before.'

Bill may have objected to getting involved with Charlotte, but he certainly rallied to the occasion. When we landed in New York he phoned a hotel for women and got her a room. We brought her there in a cab and deposited her at the front door, giving her our names and phone numbers. There was no trouble keeping in touch with her Bill ran into her unexpectedly several times during the day, and she generally turned up at my house in the evening. She stayed in New York for just over a week and then decided to go back home. We arranged for her return passage, and I telephoned her long distance the next day. She had arrived safely and was glad to be back, but she hoped to return to New York for a visit some day. Everyone had been so nice to her, and she was glad to find out that all the bad things people say about big cities are not

50

true. Charlotte and I corresponded for years after that, and I was constantly grateful for her having come into my life. In fact, it appears that the experience of Charlotte may well have been the signal for the beginning of the end of the 'magic' that had been happening so regularly for the past three months.

It was getting toward autumn and it had been a wearing summer. Bill had retained his interest in Cayce, and suggested that we might take a few days off, go down to Virginia Beach, Virginia, and look over the evidence there. The idea did not appeal to me. That sort of thing still frightened me and I did not want it to be true. It was bad enough that I did not understand what was happening to me. I particularly did not want any exacerbation of my unfortunate 'magical' efforts, which I was by now more than willing to abandon. Nevertheless, the idea of a short vacation sounded good, and my husband, knowing I was tired, encouraged me to go. It was a perfect time of the year for the trip, and he thought it would do me good. He and Bill had become friends, and although he felt Bill was developing some rather strange interests, my husband knew he would take care of me. I set out for Virginia Beach with some misgivings, but looking forward to the rest.

As it turned out the trip was anything but restful for me. The people at the Association for Research and Enlightenment, then only a small group devoted to making the Cayce material available to the public, were intelligent, sincere and obviously sane. Nor was the massive documentation something one could easily brush aside. I was impressed but very uneasy, even though Hugh Lynn Cayce, Edgar Cayce's son and head of the organization, was especially hospitable and compassionate to us. As Bill's interest deepened my own anxiety grew. Bill read further on the subject that afternoon, and he also bought some books to take home. I riffled through a volume and put it down abruptly, in sufficient discomfort to border on panic. I was glad when the trip was over. Back home I glanced at several of the books Bill had bought, but I could not read them. To me they merely seemed to sound the 'magic' note again.

My own 'magic' phase ended abruptly with a particularly clear picture episode in which I knew I had made an irrevocable choice. I saw myself entering a cave cut into a rock formation on a bleak, wind-swept seacoast. All I found in the cave was a large and very old parchment scroll. Its ends were attached to heavy gold-tipped poles, and the scroll was wrapped around them so that they met

51

in the middle of the scroll and were tied tightly together With some difficulty I managed to untie the ends and open the scroll just enough to reveal the center panel, on which two words were written: 'GOD IS.' Then I unrolled the scroll all the way. As I did so, tiny letters began to appear on both sides of the panel. The silent Voice which I had 'heard' before explained the situation mentally to me:

'If you look at the left side you will be able to read the past,' said the Voice. 'If you look at the right side you will be able to read the future.'

The little letters on the sides of the panel were becoming clearer, but I hesitated only a moment before rolling up the scroll sufficiently to conceal everything except the center panel.

'I'm not interested in reading the past or the future,' I said with finality. 'I'll just stop with this.'

The Voice sounded both reassured and reassuring.

'You made it that time,' it said. 'Thank you.'

And that, it seemed, was that."

Several times afterward Helen felt something like the subway experience of years before, although with much less intensity These occurrences generally took place in a crowd of people, and she would feel a brief but powerful affinity for them.

↶ *One summer evening, my husband and I were walking about a crowded boardwalk. A deep sense of emotional closeness to everyone there swept over me, along with a certain recognition that we were all going on the same journey to a common goal. Another time, Bill, Louis and I were at the theater together Sitting in the dark, I was aware of a strong inner light that began in the chest area and grew increasingly intense and encompassing until it seemed to radiate throughout the theater and include everyone there. My awareness of the light, which lasted for some ten minutes, was accompanied by a deep sense of peace and joy. I could hardly believe, for a time, that no one else was aware of it.*

A somewhat similar incident occurred some time later, when Bill and I were attending a meeting in southern France. Before falling asleep one evening, a sense of unbelievable strength and joy rose up in me, again beginning in the region of the chest and rising up into my head and out into my arms. For a few minutes I felt as if I could easily reach out and touch the whole world. Later, this happy experience had a fearful counterpart in the form of a star-

tlingly clear sensation of horror that I felt one night just before returning to America. I was tired, and was lying down for a brief rest before getting ready for bed. Most unexpectedly I was seized by a murderous rage so intense that I jumped up from the bed literally shaking. These two experiences were so diametrically opposed to each other that they almost seemed to represent Heaven and hell. Nor was this shocking contrast entirely unfamiliar The 'good' priestess whose only function was to help and the 'evil' priestess with her spear raised to kill had presented a somewhat similar contrast.

Only once did I actually ask for an experience to come and cheer me up, because I was feeling low. The answer came in the form of a picture of a plant nursery. I could see neat rows of very young plants, all carefully labeled and obviously well cared for Next to the plants stood a large watering can. The picture meant nothing to me, and I found it vaguely irritating.

'And much good that is,' I grumbled. 'What's so helpful about it?'

'Look where it's growing,' said the silent Voice which, by now, was no longer entirely unexpected.

'But what does it mean?' I asked, still indignant.

'Look - where - it's - growing,' repeated the Voice, slowly and very distinctly.

'Oh, all right,' I answered, still a trifle sulkily. Then I looked at the picture more carefully. The plant nursery was completely surrounded by a bleak, lifeless desert. Only the little area in which the plants were growing was moist and green.

'And now that it's finally started,' said the Voice, 'you will go on watering it, won't you?'

Almost overcome, I promised I would try.

There were also some brief periods during which shifts in time awareness took place. Perhaps the most compelling of these happened one evening while I was brushing my hair and feeling anything but inspired. It was then I saw my life represented by a golden line stretching infinitely backward and infinitely forward. There was a miniscule dip in the line which I recognized as standing for my present life. It was laughably tiny and barely noticeable. I clasped my hands in real delight.

'What can it possibly matter what happens in this little eye-blink of time?' I asked myself, in happy amazement. 'It seems too long and important while you're in it, but in less than an instant it's as if it never happened.' I was certain of this for several minutes, during which it seemed as if a great weight had been lifted from my mind. ✍

Chapter 4

All these things happened within a period of no more than a few months. One day during September 1965, Helen told Bill she felt she was about to do something very unusual. She was concerned about the feeling, because she had no idea what the "something" was going to be; all she knew was that it was going to happen soon. Since Helen had started keeping a diary immediately after her visit to Virginia Beach, Bill suggested that if she wrote down whatever occurred to her in connection with the "unusual something" she might get a clue as to what it was to be. Nothing came of her attempts at first, and she was on the verge of giving up the idea when one evening in October while sitting in her bedroom, the now-familiar inner Voice began to give her definite instructions.

She panicked, and immediately telephoned Bill. "You know that inner Voice—it won't leave me alone!"

"What is it saying?" Bill asked.

"It keeps saying, 'This is a course in miracles. Please take notes.' What am I going to do?" she pleaded.

Calmly and supportively Bill said, "Why don't you take the notes? Take them down in that shorthand you use."

"But, Bill," Helen persisted, "what if it's gibberish? Then I'll *know* I'm crazy "

"Helen, let me tell you something," he said, ignoring her remark. "Since our Rochester trip I've been doing some reading, which I haven't shared with you because you're so antagonistic to the whole subject. But there have been numbers of people—some of them very well-known people—who have had creative inspiration come through them in a mystical way Einstein claimed to get information this way; and certainly the great playwrights and what about all the mystical poets!"

"I'm not a mystical poet," she protested. "I'm a psychologist, and I don't know that I believe in this."

"Well, since you can't make it go away, why don't you take it down and bring it into the office early—before the staff arrives—and we'll go over it together "

"And if it's gibberish?"

"We'll tear it up, and no one will ever know "

"Promise, Bill?"

"Promise."

Helen hung up, went into the living room and told Louis she was going to do some work in the bedroom, and would be out shortly She closed the bedroom door, turned off the overhead light, and sat in a chair by a lamp where she allowed herself to listen. This is what she heard that first night.

This is a course in miracles. It is a required course. Only the time you take it is voluntary. Free will does not mean that you can establish the curriculum. It means only that you can elect what you want to take at a given time. The course does not aim at teaching the meaning of love, for that is beyond what can be taught. It does aim, however, at removing the blocks to the awareness of love's presence, which is your natural inheritance. The opposite of love is fear, but what is all-encompassing can have no opposite.

This course can therefore be summed up very simply in this way:
> *Nothing real can be threatened,*
> *Nothing unreal exists.*
Herein lies the peace of God.

Although the Voice wanted to continue, Helen was in a panic and she refused to listen further She quickly closed her shorthand book, and put it into the briefcase she carried back and forth to work each day Then she went into the living room and told Louis she was going to bed.

The next morning Bill got to the hospital at 7.30—a half an hour earlier than usual; he found Helen already there, in a state of great agitation.

55

"I don't know what to do, Bill; I just don't know what to do about it."

Bill suggested she read him what she had taken down and offered to type what she read since "I'm a better typist than you." This she managed to do despite some uncharacteristic stuttering. "Sounds rather interesting to me, Helen," he said. "Is that all there was?"

"No," Helen answered. "It seemed to want to go on, but I got afraid."

"How do the words come?" Bill asked.

"It's hard to describe," she answered. "It can't be an hallucination, really, because the Voice does not come from outside. It's all internal. There's no actual sound, and the words come mentally but very clearly. It's a kind of inner dictation you might say."

"Do you know what you're writing?" Bill asked, "or would you describe it as an automatic process?"

"Oh, no. It's not automatic at all; I'm perfectly aware of what I'm doing."

"Why don't you try and write some more tonight," Bill suggested. "See what happens."

"I don't think I can," she answered. "I really find it too upsetting."

Despite her reluctance to continue writing, she did not have the ability to eliminate the Voice. This became obvious that very afternoon when she was on the telephone. As soon as she hung up the receiver, the inner Voice began. She jumped up, and hurried into Bill's office to tell him what was happening. After reassuring her again that there was nothing to be frightened about, he suggested that the best thing for her to do was simply to take the words down whenever they came, and see if that were less disturbing to her than continuing to fight it.

She argued with him for almost half an hour, pointing out that this was *not* what she wanted to do. But even while she was telling Bill this, during his responses, the inner Voice would gently reappear. In desperation, Helen finally agreed to try to take the words down. "But just until I see what it is," she added.

It took less than fifteen minutes for her to get an idea of "what it is," for shortly after she returned to her desk, the voice began to dictate the first words of the Text of *A Course in Miracles.* What she heard was: "Principles of Miracles," which began,

1. *There is no order of difficulty in miracles. One is not "harder" or "bigger" than another. They are all the same. All expressions of love are maximal.*

2. *Miracles as such do not matter. The only thing that matters is their Source, Which is far beyond evaluation.*

3. *Miracles occur naturally as expressions of love. The real miracle is the love that inspired them. In this sense everything that comes from love is a miracle.*

4. *All miracles mean life, and God is the Giver of life. His Voice will direct you very specifically. You will be told all you need to know.*

5. *Miracles are habits, and should be involuntary. They should not be under conscious control. Consciously selected miracles can be misguided.*

6. *Miracles are natural. When they do not occur something has gone wrong.*

The telephone interrupted, and Helen did not hear the Voice again until that evening at home, when it continued dictating the Principles of Miracles right where it had left off, at Number 7.

That night Helen finished taking down the fifty principles of miracles that begin the Text. Even though she refused to read what she had written, she remained stunned. She did not have any idea of what *A Course in Miracles* was—it could have been just the fifty principles as far as she was concerned—but she did know that the material was coming from an unusually authoritative source—one she did not intellectually believe in.

* * * * * * *

Thus began the actual transmission of the material which Helen would take down in more than a hundred shorthand notebooks over a period of seven and a half years. The situation proved to be tremendously paradoxical. On the one hand, she resented the Voice, objected to taking down the material, was extremely fearful of the content and had to overcome great personal resistance, especially in the beginning stages, in order to continue. On the other hand, it never seriously occurred to her not to do it, even though she frequently was tremendously resentful of the often infuriating interference.

The morning after she took down the fifty principles, she met Bill at the office an hour before the staff usually arrived. Since their offices were away from the main flow of traffic in the building, thanks to Bill's choice two years previously, they did not have to be concerned with people coming by and inquiring as to what they were doing. Nevertheless, they locked the door to Bill's office every morning over the next seven and a half years, whenever they met to go over the material she had taken down the previous day

When Bill asked Helen that morning to read aloud what she had written so he could type it up, she could barely get the words out. Before she was halfway through the first sentence she began a coughing fit that lasted over five minutes. Then she had to keep clearing her throat as it seemed to be continually filling with phlegm. After more than an hour, she had been able to dictate only the first eighteen principles, and Bill had to leave to keep an appointment. They decided to try and finish the transcribing after work that day

Bill was finally able to receive the fifty principles from Helen late that afternoon, after much stuttering, stammering, yawning and coughing on her part. He gave her the original copy he had typed, while he took the carbon home with him. As he carefully read and digested what he had typed, he realized that if it were all true, then absolutely everthing he had believed in the past would be false. He was not only startled, but very apprehensive, for he recognized that if he were to take the material seriously, it would involve him in a mind shift of tremendous proportions—one which seemed to be far in excess of what he personally felt he could do. He was also aware that somehow he had asked for "a better way," and there was no question in his mind that this was the answer to his request. He had never tried to envision what that answer might be, and he certainly never would have expected that it might come in this form. He felt overwhelmed with doubts. However, he also felt a sense of obligation to at least try to suspend disbelief, for not only had he asked for it, but he recognized almost instantly the truth of many of the fifty principles. He also felt there was a vague familiarity to them, even though they contradicted his conscious belief system, and seemingly bore little resemblance to anything he had known in the past.

Bill called Helen that evening, and asked her what she felt about the fifty principles. She told him she had not re-read them, and had no interest in doing so. She said she had reluctantly agreed to take down the material, but that didn't mean she had to read it, think about it, discuss it or believe it. She added that the Voice had been dictating that evening, and it looked as though she and Bill had better adjust their schedules so they could meet regularly at his office every morning at seven o'clock.

The following morning was a repetition of the previous one. However, through the coughing, the sighing and the "inability to see my notes," Helen did manage to dictate, and Bill was able to type, everything she had taken down the previous day Bill then told Helen he had to read the material back to her since they had to be sure he had typed it correctly, and though she protested that she didn't want to hear it, she recognized the importance of what he said. So she agreed to listen:

> *Revelation induces complete but temporary suspension of doubt and fear It reflects the original form of communication between God and his creations, involving the extremely personal sense of creation sometimes sought in physical relationships. Physical closeness cannot achieve it. Miracles, however are genuinely interpersonal, and result in true closeness to other   "*

Helen interrupted, and told Bill he'd better start again. When he asked why, she answered, "I can't seem to hear the words. I can see your lips moving, but I can't hear a word you're saying." Through the years this seemed to be a rather persistent affliction that affected Helen during Bill's readings, although eventually he always managed to get through the material he had typed that day

From the very beginning, both Helen and Bill found the material very fear-promoting as it emerged, although Bill had to admit there certainly was nothing about the content that was threatening per se. The threat to his belief system, however, proved a monumental problem for him to reconcile. In addition, the religious terminology and the indicated source of the dictation were not easy for either of them to accept. Helen, a professed atheist, had no doubt the material was being given her by Jesus, for the Course was dictated in the first person, and at one point states:

> The Name of Jesus Christ as such is but a symbol.
> But it stands for love that is not of this world. It is a
> symbol that is safely used as a replacement for the
> many names of all the gods to which you pray
> This course has come from him because his words
> have reached you in a language you can love and
> understand.

By the end of the first ten days, Bill had typed fourteen pages, but when he met Helen the next morning she had no material to read him. Since neither of them had any idea of what *A Course in Miracles* was, or how long it might be, Bill wondered if the Course were completed. Helen said it wasn't, but she simply wasn't going to take any more down until she knew what it was for Bill's pragmatic response was that the only way he knew for her to get that answer was to ask the Voice. "If it doesn't tell you, it obviously doesn't want you to continue." This thought was hopeful enough to Helen so that she agreed to ask that evening. This was the answer she received:

> The world situation is worsening to an alarming
> degree. People all over the world are being called on
> to help, and are making their individual contributions
> as part of an overall prearranged plan. Part of the plan
> is taking down *A Course in Miracles*, and I am ful-
> filling my part in the agreement, as you will fulfill
> yours. You will be using abilities you developed long
> ago, and which you are not really ready to use again.
> Because of the acute emergency, however, the usual
> slow, evolutionary process is being by-passed in what
> might best be described as a "celestial speed-up."

Helen could sense the urgency that lay behind this "explanation," regardless of what she might have thought about its content. She strongly sensed that what was being conveyed to her was that time was running out. In an unusual act for her, she re-read the message, and when she finished, she knew on some level that she did not understand, she had volunteered to do this job.

That seemed so strange and bizarre to her that she was ready to throw her notebook in the trash basket, and yet it triggered something like a long ago memory in her in which she said, "Of course I'll go, Father; it's for such a little while."

Still, she was obviously not completely satisfied, for she tried one more time to abdicate her position. "Why me?" she asked. "I'm not religious; I don't understand these things; I don't even believe them. I'm about the poorest choice you could make."

The answer came back very clearly "On the contrary; you are an excellent choice. In fact, the best."

"But why?" she anguished. And then, without a hint of doubt she heard the answer· "Because you'll do it."

Helen had no response to that. She knew the Voice was right. she knew she would do it. And from that moment on the future of *A Course in Miracles* was set, Helen would "scribe" it to its completion, even though she might raise loud objections all along the way

* * * * * * *

Although there was a kind of predestination to Helen's taking down the Course, she was hardly a completely willing participant. One morning, two weeks after the "scribing" had begun, Bill removed the material he had just typed from the typewriter, and read it back to Helen according to the procedure they had previously worked out. When he had completed reading aloud, he asked her what a particular sentence meant to her She told him she hadn't heard the sentence except as individual words to be checked for accuracy, since she really had no interest in what the material meant. She then told him she thought the best way for them to handle the assignment they seemed to have undertaken together was for Bill to read the material for content, while she would check on the style and make sure the syntax and grammer were correct, since that was all she really cared about.

Although Bill knew how threatened Helen felt by all that the material implied, he also thought that Helen's intellectual curiosity would not allow her to remain so isolated from the heart of the material. He assumed that before too much time went by, her intellect would overcome her fears sufficiently so that she would indeed become as engrossed in the content as he was. As the transcribing continued, however, his assumption proved to be only partially correct, for although Helen was perfectly aware of what the material said, she remained extremely uncomfortable discussing it with Bill for nearly a year

During that time, to try and help Helen overcome her apprehensions, Bill suggested that they get in touch with Hugh Lynn Cayce of the A.R.E., and show him what Helen had taken down. Helen, of course, resisted the idea immediately, indicating that it would be dangerous for their careers to show the material to anyone. After weeks of reassuring her, however, Bill finally got her to agree that it might indeed be helpful to know what Hugh Lynn thought of the material, since his work had brought him into contact with many similar paranormal experiences. Helen finally agreed to let Bill show him what she had taken down on the condition that their meeting would be completely confidential.

In Bill's continuing search for knowledge about the paranormal, he had remained in touch with the A.R.E., and so it was easy for him to arrange a meeting with Hugh Lynn, with whom he had remained in phone contact since the time he and Helen had visited Virginia Beach.

They met in New York, during one of Hugh Lynn's visits to the city, and Helen brought along almost everything she had thus far taken down. Since Bill had told him on the phone much of the background behind Helen's writing, very little had to be said about it, and after a few pleasantries, Hugh Lynn asked if he could look through the manuscript while they were together As he leafed through the pages, Hugh Lynn became more and more engrossed, and his comments indicated he was indeed impressed.

After a while, he put the manuscript down, and shook his head in amazement. "Remarkable," he said; "it's absolutely inspired." He went on to tell them he felt parts of it were quite similar to the more spiritual portions of his father's trance readings.

Since Bill had previously spoken to Hugh Lynn about Helen's "discomfort" regarding what was happening to her, Hugh Lynn made a special point of telling Helen that he was well aware of what an overwhelming job she was doing, and assuring her that he knew how difficult it must be for her "However," he said, "you seem to have been chosen to do this, because you're obviously a very advanced soul. I only wish you could see yourself as I do."

Although the meeting with Hugh Lynn did not relieve Helen of her apprehensions, his support did seem to comfort her somewhat, and she did continue the work, if not with a great deal of ease, at least with somewhat less un-ease.

* * * * * * *

The Voice would dictate to Helen almost daily, and sometimes several times a day The timing never conflicted with work or social activities, starting at some time when she was reasonably free to write without interference. As a result she began to carry her short-hand notebook with her almost everywhere she went "just in case."

That in itself, of course, was no guarantee that she would do the job without protesting. She could, and very often did, refuse to cooperate, at least initially But she soon discovered she could have no peace until she relented and joined in once again. Depsite being aware of this, she still sometimes refused to write for extended periods. When this occurred, it was usually at Louis' urging that she did return to work, for he knew full well that she could only eliminate her distress by resuming her function as Course "scribe," and he was able to convince her that to continue fighting the inevitable could only have a deleterious effect on their relationship.

Evenings turned out to be a favored time for the Voice to dictate. Helen objected bitterly to this, as the writing was in no way automatic, and always required her full cooperation, and she resented her evenings being impinged on. Often, in a fit of defiance, she would go to bed without writing anything. When she did this she couldn't sleep, and would eventually get up in disgust and write as directed. Sometimes she was so tired that she went back to bed and fell asleep after taking down only a few paragraphs. However, she would be impelled to continue with the section before breakfast the next morning, perhaps finishing it on her way to work or at odd moments between work pressures during the day She never knew when she started a sentence how it would end, and the ideas came so quickly that she had trouble keeping up with them, even though she used a combination of shorthand symbols and abbreviations she had developed during years of taking class notes and recording therapy sessions.

The writing was highly interruptable. At the office she could lay the notebook down to answer the telephone, talk to a patient, supervise a junior staff member, or attend to one of numerous emergencies, and then return to the writing without even checking back to see where she had left off. At home she could talk to Louis, chat with a friend or take a nap, going back to the notebook afterwards without disturbing the flow of words in the slightest. It did not matter whether she had stopped at the end of a paragraph or in the middle of a sentence. It was as if the Voice merely waited until she came back, and then started in again. She wrote with equal ease at home, or in the office, on a park bench, or in a taxi, bus or subway The presence of other people did not interfere at all. When the time for writing came, external circumstances simply appeared to be irrelevant.

Neither Helen nor Bill had any idea, of course, how much material there was going to be, and after two months of listening and writing, Helen asked how long the Text would be. The answer she received was that she would know when the Text was completed because she would hear the final "Amen."

This seemed to be a particularly frustrating answer for Helen, and she told Bill if that was the kind of cooperative response she was going to get, then she was just going to forget the whole thing. Bill did not argue with her, and merely said that if she changed her mind to let him know and he would arrange to be at the office early so they could go over the material as they had been doing.

Helen went home that night determined not to listen to the Voice. She did not sleep well at all, and was extremely irritable the next day at the hospital. Bill said nothing to her about the Course, discussing only those matters that concerned her research work and the project in which she was involved.

Three days went by before Helen was willing to acknowledge that her sleeplessness and distress were obviously connected with her refusing to take down what she was continuing to hear Finally, at 3 AM she picked up her notebook, and the Voice resumed exactly where it had left off three days earlier

This episode turned out to be one that recurred intermittently Despite the fact that Helen recognized that when she refused to take down the Course she became highly depressed, she nevertheless, threatened to resign periodically Although her longest period of withdrawal was nearly a month, Bill never seriously considered that she wouldn't complete her assignment. And basically, she knew her "temper tantrums" were merely a delaying tactic too.

As the material continued to flow, and Bill continued to study it, he realized he had almost no background in spiritual or mystical writings, and that he was vastly unfamiliar with many of the references to which the Course alluded. He had always associated spiritual teachings with formal religion, and was unfamiliar with mystical tradition. He recognized, therefore, that in order for him to be able to consider and evaluate the Course seriously he would have to give himself a cram course not only in the world's religions, but also in mystical practices, for it was apparent to him that although the Course was not a religion, it did have a basic metaphysical foundation.

Thus he immediately began to read as avidly as possible all of the books he could find that might be related in some way or another with mystical disciplines. In the process he compiled a vast library of material, a collection that he tried sharing with Helen, who would have no part of it. Although she told him she was not interested in reading mystical material, it was clear that she was glad he was doing so. For the more he told her about what he was learning, the more reassured she was that what they were doing was not odd, but was indeed consistent with the most profound philosophical and spiritual teachings of the ages, both East and West.

About six weeks after they had begun their morning typing sessions, Helen noticed that Bill put two carbons into the typewriter instead of the usual one. When she asked him why, he told her that a colleague had expressed an interest many months before in discussing religious matters with him. At that time, Bill had told him he had no interest in religion or the spiritual search and that he therefore had nothing to discuss. "Now, though," Bill told Helen, "I feel John should know about this and that we should share the material with him."

Helen immediately and vehemently opposed the idea. What they were doing, she indicated, was highly suspect psychologically, people would think she was crazy and both their jobs would be jeopardized if any of their colleagues ever found out. Bill assured her that John was deeply interested in the philosophy of religion, that no one was going to "find out" and that discussing the material with John would prove to be of enormous benefit to both himself and Helen. Despite her continued misgivings, he managed to persuade her that it was something he should do.

That morning Bill went to John's office, and told him everything that had been happening. John was intrigued, and was eager to begin sharing the material.

At eight o'clock every morning, from then on, John would come to Bill's office where Bill would give him the second carbon of the material he had typed the day before; Bill would then read it aloud, and they would discuss it for as long as their schedules would allow John, who had been brought up as a Southern Baptist, had read extensively on the subject of religion and his input to the discussions was of great aid to Bill in helping him put the material into perspective.

The more Bill read, and the more he discussed the material with John, the more he realized that the Course was inspired, profound and extremely beneficial in helping one heal the relationships that might be causing one pain. As the Text continued to grow in length, he recognized that here indeed was the help he had asked for— material that indicated how he could achieve a "better way" of living in the world.

The first place to begin was obviously with Helen. If they could make some progress in the way they got along with each other, then he knew other relationships could be healed as well. However, when he suggested, tentatively, that the material might help them improve their relationship, her reaction was anything but tentative.

She began to chide him for being so naive, and she accused him of having all of the faults and shortcomings she had always seen in him. Bill reacted in knee-jerk fashion, accusing and finding fault in exactly the way he had done over the past several years.

But then he remembered his purpose in bringing up the subject in the first place, and he stopped both attacking and defending. And within a short period of time Helen had at least agreed to discuss some of the concepts of the Course with him, the goal being not only to fully understand the concepts, but also to put them into practice in their daily lives.

It was not an easy task. Helen's resistance to discussing the material was still enormous, and although Bill cared deeply for her, he still was unable to look past those aspects of her behavior and personality that were so irritating to him. This did not mean there was no improvement in their relationship. Indeed, there was what could truly be called a "miraculous" improvement that occurred whenever they were involved with anything having to do with taking down the Course. During these times, there was never any friction, never any conflicts, nothing but cooperation between them. It was as if they were joined in producing something extraordinarily sacred something which did not allow for the usual personality conflicts to interfere. And when they had shared a particularly beautiful and affecting passage of the Course, that was a time when the relationship seemed truly healed.

The first time this occurred was when they had reached what would eventually prove to be the mid-point in the Text. One night Helen was taking down what she heard from the Voice, when she realized what she was hearing made no sense at all. She became extremely agitated, for her immediate fear was that she had finally lost her sanity She protested to the Voice, indicating that what it was saying was senseless, but the Voice merely reacted by calmly telling her to take down what she heard, assuring her that in the morning she would understand the words perfectly well. She was not reassured, but she did indeed take the words down as she heard them, even though she was sure what she was writing was pure gibberish.

When she met Bill in the morning, she told him her worst fears   that even though she had been reassured to the contrary by the Voice, she was certain that what she was about to read him would make no sense at all.

After dictating to Bill what she had taken down the previous night, he read it back, and Helen listened with a mixture of concern and trepidation. This is what Bill read:

> *Forgive us our illusions, Father, and help us to accept our true relationship with You, in which there are no illusions, and where none can ever enter Our holiness is Yours. What can there be in us that needs forgiveness when Yours is perfect? The sleep of forgetfulness is only the unwillingness to remember your forgiveness and Your Love. Let us not wander into temptation, for the temptation of the Son of God is not Your Will. And let us receive only what You have given, and accept but this into the minds which you created and which You love. Amen.*

Bill was barely able to finish without his voice cracking. He looked across at Helen, and was astonished to see her burst into tears. Instantaneously they each recognized that what Helen had been unwilling to comprehend the night before was clearly the Course's version of the Lord's Prayer And though neither said a word, each felt a unity with the other that had never been felt before.

* * * * * * *

The scribing of the Text continued for more than another year, and during this time Bill continued trying to use the principles of the Course in dealing with *all* his relationships. Although his department was still underfunded, and there was still no clear channel of authority for him to use to try to improve conditions, his personal relationships at the hospital—along with the relationships of the members of the staff with each other—improved dramatically There was a great deal more cooperation and much less competitiveness, and a generally pleasant atmosphere prevailed. Without any question, Bill attributed this to the help he received from his determination to see things differently, as the Course was teaching him.

And yet there was still one area in which he was unable to see permanent positive results, and that was in his on-going relationship with Helen. Whether they were working on a research paper, writing a grant proposal or merely having lunch together, which they did every work day, they still seemed unable or unwilling to see each other differently than the way they had in the past. Hours could be spent angrily criticizing each other's writing, each other's friendships, each other's habits, and still, paradoxically, each also was able to provide the other with greatly needed help in both their professional work and in their personal lives. For without many of Helen's suggestions concerning administrative details, which Bill would finally, though reluctantly, accept, Bill would never have been able to improve the efficiency of the department to the extent he did. And without Bill's constant professional support, Helen would have been unable to remain at the hospital and do the excellent clinical work she did.

While Bill seemed to be seeing positive results in the way his "difficult" relationships were progressing, Helen seemed to have a much harder time in trying to put the principles into practice. This was undoubtedly due to her inability to completely let go of her basic resistance to taking down the material. Throughout the writing—which spanned a period of over seven years—the acute terror she felt at the beginning did gradually recede, but part of Helen's mind simply never allowed her to get completely used to the idea of being a channel for the Voice. And although there were times when she felt curiously transported as she wrote, those times were widely spaced and usually brief. For the most part she was bleakly unbelieving, suspicious and afraid.

Throughout, however, in this one area, she did have the complete and unquestioning support of Bill, who comforted her at her most fearful times, and humored her when she was most obstinate. In addition, her husband's attitude was unexpectedly helpful. After Helen had been writing at home for a few weeks, Louis had asked her what she was working on. With considerable misgivings she decided to tell him the truth. His reaction was more than tolerant. He was actually encouraging. Although it was evident at the start that the content disturbed him (and she therefore stopped showing him the material) he actually encouraged her involvement, and unlike Helen, did not find the process itself anxiety producing. Without the support of these two men, it is obvious she could not possibly have done the job.

At the time that Helen had begun to feel less uncomfortable with the content of the material, she found herself now and then changing various words that she felt were inconsistent with the basic concepts of the material that she had been taking down. Usually the urge to change them back to the original was so strong that she did so within days. If she didn't, the matter was apt to disturb her until she did. Furthermore, it quickly became apparent to her that the original words were not chosen at random, but were indeed very carefully selected. Sometimes what seemed to Helen to be inconsistent at first, was explained later, and the original wording was necessary for the sake of subsequent clarity At other times specifically worded ideas were referred to later in contexts of which she had not originally been aware, so that changes she was tempted to make would have eventually reduced the consistency of the thoughts rather than enhanced it, had her own feelings prevailed.

One day, about two years after she had started scribing the Course, Helen began to be aware that much of the material she was then taking down had a poetic nature to it. Glancing through the more recently transcribed pages of her notebook, she said to Bill that a good deal of the recent material was written in blank verse—iambic pentameter, Shakespearean style. "How much of what we've already done do you suppose is written the same way, Bill?" she wondered. "I just love poetry "

Bill took out the five hundred or so pages of typed manuscript, and started leafing through it, and to his amazement, many of the parts he looked at were written in the same poetic meter He couldn't believe that he had been listening to, typing and reading this material for so many months without noticing such a thing, and so that night he went back to the very beginning, and began to read to himself. The initial material certainly was written in prose, and he wondered where the change had taken place. He thumbed through the pages, scanning quickly and hurrying on, until he detected where indeed the material seemed to slide in and out of blank verse—a short way back. And as he re-read the words, the newly recognized rhythm of many of the passages seemed to make the material even more beautiful and inspirational. He called Helen on the phone, told her what he had learned and read her a sample:

> Let us be still an instant, and forget
> all things we ever learned, all thoughts we had,
> and every preconception that we hold
> of what things mean and what their purpose is.
> Let us remember not our own ideas
> of what the world is for We do not know.
> Let every image held of everyone
> be loosened from our minds and swept away.

She seemed deeply pleased and gratified, and after a short silence merely said, "Isn't that lovely, Bill; isn't that lovely "

In September 1968, three years and nine hundred and forty-four typewritten pages after she had begun taking down what the Voice was dictating, Helen heard and transcribed the following·

> In joyous welcome is my hand outstretched to every brother who would join with me in reaching past temptation, and who looks with fixed determination toward the light that shines beyond in perfect constancy. Give me my own, for they belong to You. And can You fail in what is but Your Will? I give You thanks for what my brothers are. And as each one elects to join with me, the song of thanks from earth to Heaven grows from tiny scattered threads of melody to one inclusive chorus from a world redeemed from hell, and giving thanks to You.
>
> And now we say "Amen." For Christ has come to dwell in the abode You set for Him before time was, in calm eternity. The journey closes. ending at the place where it began. No trace of it remains. Not one illusion is accorded faith, and not one spot of darkness still remains to hide the face of Christ from anyone. Thy Will is done. complete and perfectly. and all creation recognizes You, and knows You as the only Source it has. Clear in Your likeness does the Light shine forth from everything that lives and moves in You. For we have reached where all of us are one. and we are home. where You would have us be.

Helen put down her notebook, picked up the phone in her bedroom and dialed. With a sense of quiet reverence she said, "Bill, *A Course in Miracles* is completed."

Helen, of course, did not know she was mistaken when she told Bill she had completed receiving the Course, for neither she nor Bill had any idea of what *A Course in Miracles* actually was. Bill, who had been avidly reading everything even remotely connected with mysticism and metaphysics, knew that what they now had in their possession was a spiritual document that was very closely related to the teachings of the non-dualistic Vedanta of the Hindu religion, and that the profundity of the Vedanta certainly paralleled the obvious profundity of the Course. He realized the basic spiritual teachings of both had many striking similarities to each other, and that the main difference between them was that the Course was stating the perennial philosophy of eternal truths in Christian terminology with a psychological application that seemed expressly aimed at a contemporary audience.

He also knew that the almost nine hundred and fifty typewritten pages they had accumulated contained the answer to the question he had asked almost three years before, that there must be a better way to live in the universe. The Course, he knew, was his answer, and although it was difficult to explain to himself how it happened, he felt strongly that it did happen because two people had made the conscious commitment to join for a common purpose. And in that non-judgmental joining, something miraculous occurred.

The Course had also proved to be extremely practical for him. His professional relationships had certainly changed and become more peaceful. And those personal relationships with which he had been having difficulty had also become more satisfactory. Only his relationship with Helen had been a disappointment, for though he thought he wanted the relationship to be peaceful, he had thus far been unable to let that happen.

The day after Helen called Bill to tell him the Course was completed, they met in his office before lunch. Bill unlocked the filing cabinet where he kept the material, and he put the six file folders that contained the manuscript on his desk.

"We really should put these into a more substantial folder," he said "I'll look for something suitable during the lunch hour "

When Bill returned, he was carrying a few large black binders—the kind used by their doctoral students to secure their theses '

"These are all I could find that were large enough to hold the material," he said to Helen As he secured the pages, he asked, "Well, Helen, what do we do now?"

"Do? What do you mean 'do?' We don't do anything You're not thinking of showing it to anyone, are you?" she asked apprehensively

"I'm not thinking of doing anything, Helen, but I don't really believe we went through almost three years of this just to keep it locked in a filing cabinet "

"As far as I'm concerned, that would be fine with me," she answered

"Why don't you ask what we should do?" Bill suggested

The Voice was an authority for whom Helen had developed a great deal of respect, and she told Bill she thought that his suggestion was a good one, and that she would ask at home that night In the meantime though, she wanted to be sure Bill agreed with her that they should not show the material to anyone

Bill of course agreed, for he felt as well as Helen did that their academic reputations would come under a great deal of suspicion if the true story of the Course were to be divulged

The next morning Helen met Bill at his office, and said the Voice had been very clear when she had asked: they were to do nothing at this time She was obviously relieved

Bill spent what spare time he had available during the next month carefully reading and re-reading the material He was particularly impressed with the absolute consistency of the work, noting that he could find not a single conflicting passage or idea throughout its entire length He was confused, however, about what kind of a "course" this was supposed to be, for the manuscript, as typed, contained over two hundred and fifty thousand words, with not one chapter, or sub-chapter break, and he felt that run-on material presented in such a formidable way as this, regardless of how inspirational it was, would attract very few readers Perhaps, he thought, the real purpose of the Course might very well be to merely present the message to Helen and himself for them to use Yet he could not really convince himself of this, for he felt the Voice could not have given so much knowledge just for the benefit of two people who were struggling with their relationships. That didn't make sense to him at all. He finally recognized that since he had asked for a better way, and it had been given to him, that he was simply to *use* it, and not worry about what to *do* with it.

Chapter 5

From September 1968, when Helen had "completed" scribing the Course, until the following spring, she and Bill found themselves deeply involved in several new projects at the hospital. Then, one day early in May, during lunch she said, "You know, Bill, I thought I was so relieved when the Text was finished, but strange as it seems I really miss my function." During the next several days she became increasingly restless. "I don't know what it is Bill," she said with some distraction, "but I think there's going to be something like a work book."

Two weeks later the Voice returned, and they learned that the Text Helen had received over the past three years was not the entire Course, as they had each thought, and that the forthcoming Workbook for Students was to be an integral part of *A Course in Miracles*. Helen was not happy; for all she knew the Workbook could turn out to be twice as long as the Text, and the dictation could go on for five years or more.

When the Voice began dictating though, those fears were quickly dispelled, for the first two paragraphs that Helen took down told her precisely what they had to look forward to:

> *A theoretical foundation such as the text provides is necessary as a framework to make the exercises in this workbook meaningful. Yet it is doing the exercises that will make the goal of the course possible. An untrained mind can accomplish nothing. It is the purpose of this workbook to train your mind to think along the lines the text sets forth.*

> *The exercises are very simple They do not require*
> *a great deal of time, and it does not matter where*
> *you do them They need no preparation The train-*
> *ing period is one year The exercises are numbered*
> *1 to 365 Do not undertake to do more than one set*
> *of exercises a day*

Helen was a lot less resistant to scribing the Workbook than she had been to the Text This could have been due to the fact that she was now accustomed to the Voice, but it was also probably due to the content of the introductory instructions to the Workbook Just prior to receiving Lesson 1, Helen took down the following:

> *Remember only this: you need not believe the ideas,*
> *you need not accept them, and you need not even*
> *welcome them Some of them you may actively*
> *resist None of this will matter, or decrease their ef-*
> *ficacy But do not allow yourself to make exceptions*
> *in applying the ideas the workbook contains, and*
> *whatever your reactions to the ideas may be, use*
> *them Nothing more than that is required*

The fact that the Voice gave specific permission not to believe the lessons if one so desired, was quite a relief to Helen She thus did not have to face the many ideological conflicts that the content of the Text presented to her In addition, Helen's resistance was lessened because she did recognize that by putting the principles of the Course into practice, relationships at the hospital had become much less stressful, Thus, being extremely pragmatic, she could hardly choose to argue with the basic ideas of that which seemed to be helping so much

The first lessons that were dictated were quite compact, and this too had a positive effect on Helen's attitude, for she knew there would be only three hundred and sixty-five lessons, and she could see, with the way the first lessons were being structured, that taking down the Workbook would not be nearly as long a job as the Text had turned out to be Of course the lessons did get longer, but by the time Helen noticed, she was so absorbed with the way they were developing that she almost stopped complaining altogether about the intrusion of the Voice into her life

It took twenty-one months before the dictation of the Workbook was completed During that time the friendlier, less competitive attitudes of their professional associates, which began to become manifest when Bill first started to apply the principles of the Course, continued to proliferate This, Bill felt, would have been remarkable under the best of conditions, but what was more miraculous to him was that the feelings continued to grow even during periods of tremendous work pressure and personal frustration that seemed to be endemic to working within the hospital's organizational structure

When the Voice reached Lesson 365 in February 1971, Helen said a silent prayer of thanks, for she once again felt her work was completed Even the epilogue that followed the final lesson indicated to her that her function as a "scribe" had been finished, for it began this way:

> *This course is a beginning, not an end   No more*
> *specific lessons are assigned, for there is no more*
> *need of them*

And it concluded with the words:

> *We trust our ways to Him and say "Amen " In peace*
> *we will continue in His way, and trust all things to*
> *Him In confidence we wait His answers, as we ask*
> *His Will in everything we do He loves God's Son as*
> *we would love him And he teaches us how to behold*
> *him through His eyes, and love him as He does You*
> *do not walk alone God's angels hover near and all*
> *about His Love surrounds you, and of this be sure;*
> *that I will never leave you comfortless*

When the Workbook was done, Bill observed that its clarity and progressive organization impressed him even more than the Text, because in gently leading one to a higher level of awareness, the lessons were so psychologically sound that only a master psychologist could have thought them up

Despite their professional awareness of the transcendent quality of the material, and the effectiveness of its concepts, neither Helen nor Bill had any idea about what they should do with the Course, aside from reading it, studying it and trying to practice it They felt that at some point in time it would have to be shared, but they had no idea as to when or how They did not, however, concern themselves about it, for their experience with the Course's teachings led them to know that at the appropriate time their internal guidance would lead them to the correct decision concerning the destiny of the material.

The Course, meanwhile, was making a difference in their lives. In many ways it was now more difficult for them to return to old patterns of working and relating to others. For if they did, they each experienced an increasing sense of discomfort. Their frustration at such times often became so great that interactions which previously had caused them to experience conflict now produced even greater strain.

In the summer of 1971 Bill told Helen that his feelings about "doing something" to make the material more readable had become much more intense, and he asked her if she would be willing to go through the Text with him, and ask for help in making it less formidable to the eye. Helen agreed to ask if this should be done, and the answer she received was a very clear affirmative.

Thus began a project that was almost as time consuming as was the original scribing of the material. Whenever they had free time, and almost every Saturday afternoon, Helen and Bill read slowly through the Text, feeling and asking where the natural breaks might occur In this manner, over a fourteen month period, the Text was broken down into thirty-one chapters with two hundred and fifty-five separate sub-chapter headings.

In April 1972, while they were still working on "sub-heading" the Text, Helen came into Bill's office and almost resignedly anounced that the Voice had returned the night before, and told her she was to take down a Manual for Teachers. She had no idea what that was going to be, but experience by then led them both to know that if they had patience they would find out quickly enough.

The following morning when Helen arrived at the office she said to Bill, "Well, it looks as if A Course in Miracles still isn't completed." When he asked her what she meant, she opened one of her shorthand notebooks and read him part of what she had taken down the night before:

The role of teaching and learning is actually reversed in the thinking of the world. The reversal is characteristic. It seems as if the teacher and the learner are separated, the teacher giving something to the learner rather than to himself. Further, the act of teaching is regarded as a special activity, in which one engages only a relatively small proportion of one's time. The course, on the other hand, emphasizes that to teach is to learn, so that teacher and learner are the same. It also emphasizes that teaching is a constant process; it goes on every moment of the day, and continues into sleeping thoughts as well.

She then turned past three or four pages of her notebook until she reached the part she specifically wanted to read to him:

This is a manual for the teachers of God. They are not perfect, or they would not be here. Yet it is their mission to become perfect here, and so they teach perfection over and over, in many, many ways, until they have learned it. And then they are seen no more, although their thoughts remain a source of strength and truth forever Who are they? How are they chosen? What do they do? How can they work out their own salvation and the salvation of the world? This manual attempts to answer these questions.

She closed the notebook, and with hardly any emotion in her voice said to Bill, "I guess the sub-heading can wait."

Although Bill did not look forward to more months—or years—of typing the material Helen might take down, he was inwardly overjoyed at Helen's reaction to the situation. He knew by her comparative calmness that a real change had taken place in her attitude; she showed no signs of the kind of panic she had shown before, and although she certainly wasn't enthusiastic about resuming her role as "scribe," the fears she had exhibited previously were in no way manifest. Bill felt this in itself was a miracle, and he realized that if this change in Helen's attitude could be credited to her working with the Course's lessons, then whatever additional time he might need to devote in order to complete the job of transcribing the material, would not only be worth any sacrifices he might have to make, but would actually be a privilege to give.

The Manual for Teachers turned out to be seventy-seven typewritten pages long, and in September 1972 Helen scribed the following:

> This manual is not intended to answer all questions that both teacher and pupil may raise. In fact, it covers only a few of the more obvious ones, in terms of a brief summary of some of the major concepts in the text and workbook. It is not a substitute for either, but merely a supplement. While it is called a manual for teachers, it must be remembered that only time divides teacher and pupil, so that the difference is temporary by definition. In some cases, it may be helpful for the pupil to read the manual first. Others might do better to begin with the workbook. Still others may need to start at the more abstract level of the text.

She took down more that night, and in the morning when she got to the office she read it all to Bill, concluding with:

> And now in all your doings be you blessed.
> God turns to you for help to save the world.
> Teacher of God, His thanks He offers you,
> And all the world stands silent in the grace
> You bring from Him. You are the Son He loves,
> And it is given you to be the means
> Through which His Voice is heard around the world,
> To close all things of time; to end the sight
> Of all things visible; and to undo
> All things that change. Through you is ushered in
> A world unseen, unheard, yet truly there.
> Holy are you, and in your light the world
> Reflects your holiness, for you are not
> Alone and friendless. I give thanks for you,
> And join your efforts on behalf of God,
> Knowing they are on my behalf as well,
> And for all those who walk to God with me.
> *AMEN*

When she finished, both Bill and Helen once again felt that *A Course in Miracles* was now complete. This time they were correct.

Helen in New York City, 1917

Helen, Age 18

Helen and Louis Schucman at the time of their marriage

Bill Thetford, 1983

Helen and Bill, 1976

*Columbia University, School of Physicians & Surgeons
where Helen & Bill worked*

photo by Kathleen A. Karp

Helen with Judy Skutch, 1976

Helen with Ken Wapnick, 1977

Helen with Jerry Jampolsky, 1976

Chapter 6

Between September 1972, when the scribing of the Course was completed, and the following March, Bill showed the material to just four people—Hugh Lynn Cayce, a Catholic priest named Father Michael, who was a student in one of the graduate psychology courses Bill taught, and two close personal friends.

Each of these people had positive, but differing, reactions to the Course. The two friends found the material intellectually interesting, but had no desire to work with the lessons. Hugh Lynn felt the work was "tremendously important," and that its content indicated to him that the Course had the potential for changing "millions of lives." The priest, whose background included the study of religion and mysticism, found the Course to be completely in harmony with the great mystical teachings of the East, and felt that the lessons were brilliantly conceived.

Since Bill had had a difficult time convincing Helen to let him show the Course to each of those four people, he did not feel like going through any more discussions of that kind, and so he didn't think further about showing it to others. The Course thus went back into the filing cabinet, safely locked away for whatever the future was to hold.

In September, when the Course was completed, Bill read, in a professional journal, an article entitled "Mysticism and Schizophrenia" by Kenneth Wapnick, Ph.D. Bill knew the article would fascinate Father Michael, and so he passed it along to him, and thought nothing more of it. Father Michael, however, did a lot of thinking about the ideas in the article, and about the author

* * * * * *

Kenneth Wapnick was thirty years old, and had received his doctorate in psychology four years previously He had been born and raised in the Jewish faith, but in mid-1972 had had a profound mystical experience which had led him to "know" that he was to become Catholic. As such, in October of that year he was officially baptized. The priest who baptized him evidently felt such high regard for his new convert that he told his friend, Father Michael, from whom he was taking a course at the time, of the beautiful baptism he had performed with "a psychologist named Dr Wapnick."

The name struck Father Michael immediately, and he told the priest he would very much like to meet Ken Wapnick. The priest said he would be delighted to introduce them, but that Dr Wapnick was considering leaving for Israel, and he didn't know what Ken's time schedule was. He said, however, he would give Michael's phone number to Ken, and do his best to get the two of them together

A few days later Ken called Michael and they made a date to meet. There was an immediate affinity between them, and they became fast friends. In the course of their many meaningful discussions about psychology and mysticism, Father Michael mentioned that he thought Ken would enjoy meeting two psychologist friends of his, but it wasn't until a few nights before he was to leave for Israel that Michael introduced him to Helen and Bill.

The four of them met at Bill's apartment after dinner The conversation was predominantly about professional matters and theories, but at one point Bill did mention the material that Helen had taken down, and asked Ken if he would be interested in looking at it. When Ken saw the voluminous size of the manuscript, he politely demurred, indicating that since he was leaving in a few days, he simply didn't have enough time to look through it in the way that he would like to.

When Ken arrived in Israel, however, he found himself thinking a great deal about the manuscript that Bill had mentioned to him. He didn't know why it kept coming into his thoughts, but it did, and he knew that when he returned to the United States, he would have to seek Bill out and have a careful look to see what the manuscript was all about.

Ken Wapnick spent over five months in Israel, including three and a half months in a Trappist monastery, and about five weeks in a monastery that was literally on a mountaintop in lower Galilee. The latter was formed to develop a community where Moslems, Christians and Jews would live and pray together The Mass was said in Hebrew, as were community prayers, and Ken was unusually happy there. He thought that perhaps this would be his final destination. However in May 1973 he felt guided to return to the United States. Although the guidance was simply that he should return, three reasons did suggest themselves to him: to heal relationships with his family, to renew relations with friends and to see the manuscript Bill had mentioned to him a few days before he left New York, and which had remained in his thoughts throughout his time in Israel.

When he returned to New York Ken had no idea how long he would remain in the States, for his feelings were that the trip was a visit, and that he was to go back to Israel, perhaps to live in a monastery for an indefinite period of time. Father Michael picked him up at the airport, and one of the first things Ken told his friend was that he would like to see Bill Thetford and the manuscript that Bill had shown him. Just five days later Bill handed him the 1500-page manuscript, Ken then discovered it was called *A Course in Miracles.*

Ken did little the next two and a half months except read the Course. During this time his feelings grew stronger and stronger that his spiritual life was to be connected in some way with the material, and that he was not to return to Israel on a permanent, or even extended, basis. When he had finally finished reading the entire Course, his sense of direction was clear· he was to go back to Israel for a short period in order to tie up the loose ends he had left there, and he was then to return to New York and somehow work with Helen and Bill and the Course.

He also felt it was important for Helen and Bill to visit Israel, and he suggested that they come over while he was there, and that he could then show them what he felt would be the meaningful sights.

Both Helen and Bill had vacation time coming to them, and since each felt an inclination to visit the Holy Land, they decided that Ken's invitation to act as guide was one that could help give their trip an added dimension they might otherwise not be able to experience.

And so in the third week of August 1973, a month after Ken had returned to Israel, and despite Helen's apprehensions about the legendary Israeli summer heat, Bill, Helen and Louis boarded an El Al jet for Tel Aviv

Although she continually complained about the "unbearable temperature," Helen participated fully in the experiences to which Ken exposed them. Especially affecting to her was her experience at Qumran, the site of the discovery of the Dead Sea scrolls.

As they approached the actual area where the scrolls had been found, Helen abruptly stopped, visibly shaken. She stared at the opening of the cave, and suddenly burst into tears. Although Bill and Louis tried desperately to comfort her, she was unable to speak for almost five minutes. When she finally regained her composure, she spoke so quietly that the others had to strain to hear her

"This is the cave," she said in a tremulous voice; "this is the cave where I saw the scroll that said 'GOD IS' " None of the others said a word; there was nothing to say

A short while later, as they were breathing in the historical atmosphere of the Dead Sea surroundings, Helen began musing half to herself. "You know," she said, "something's wrong with the water level. It's too low; it used to be much higher " Bill, who took none of Helen's thoughts lightly, opened a guide book he had bought when they had arrived in Israel, and began thumbing through it. "Very interesting, Helen," he remarked. "It says here that at the time of the Essenes, the water level of the Dead Sea was a good deal higher " Everyone was silent, and finally Helen, visibly moved, remarked quietly, "This is the holiest place on earth."

After several moments they resumed moving about, and a few minutes later, in the same area, while walking past some relics, Helen once again abruptly stopped.

She looked across a slight depression in the terrain and stared at an ancient graveyard. "There's something very familiar about that," she said. "I want to go over there and look." But before she could take even two steps, the Voice that she had become used to suddenly spoke to her "Let the dead bury the dead," the Voice said. And Helen halted, knowing full well what that meant.

Her experiences in Israel, as emotionally strong as they appeared to be, did not, in the long run, have any noticeable effect on Helen's attitude about God, reincarnation or any other spiritual matter She could not deny the impact of her experiences, but her beliefs and ideas relating to God remained as inconclusive as ever

Helen, Louis, Bill and Ken returned to New York together in the beginning of September Although Bill had indicated to Ken over the past months that it was extremely doubtful there would be an opening in the department for him, Ken's instincts nevertheless directed him to go to the Medical Center Since he had saved a modest amount of money, and since he planned on living in an inexpensive Catholic hotel on Manhattan's West Side, Ken felt that his actions, for the near future anyway, did not have to depend on his having a paid job, and the pull that he felt from the manuscript was so great that he knew he had to be involved with it no matter what obstacles might seem to be in the way

And so in mid-September 1973 Ken began going to the Medical Center every day, even though there was no official job for him to do. He spent each day carefully reading and re-reading each section of the Course, and then discussing with Helen his feelings about what he thought should be done in order to make certain that the material was absolutely clear It was a labor that could only have been done through total dedication and love. Well over a thousand hours were spent determining the precise punctuation to be used and what should or should not be capitalized. Also, Ken spent great amounts of time reviewing and refining the section breaks and headings that Helen and Bill had inserted the previous year For though Helen and Bill had done the initial work of breaking the manuscript into sections, neither of them felt completely satisfied with the job they had done. Ken therefore took it upon himself to get Helen to work with him to make sure the Course headings were in perfect harmony with the purity of the Course's content. When they couldn't agree on a matter, Ken and Helen would ask for guidance, and the answers each received always coincided.

Although Ken made no effort to augment his income by seeking private patients, three months after he began working with Helen, Father Michael referred two priests to him for counseling. This was the beginning of a modest private practice that Ken was to build up, simply by referrals, and by the fall of 1974 he was spending each Friday with clients who had sought him out for psychological counseling.

At this time, Bill also found a part-time position for Ken as a psychologist in his department. This was a particularly fortuitous piece of timing, for Ken's savings had just about run out, and he was beginning to wonder what to do about that.

As Christmas 1974 approached, Ken felt an intense inner pressure to get the editing job completed. He did not know why he felt so driven, and it certainly was not easy for him, because the more he pushed Helen to work with him, the more she seemed to resist. And yet he knew he had to persist, and he knew they had to get it done. And so evenings, week-ends and whatever other time he could get Helen to cooperate were spent in finishing the mammoth job for which he had taken responsibility

By the end of January the work was done to each one's complete satisfaction, and the manuscript that had originally been 500,000 words of run-on copy was now a self-study course that was easy to read and consistent in style. Helen, Bill and Ken felt a sense of relief that was distinctive to each one's particular personality and attitude. Helen finally felt a sense of freedom; Bill knew they had done their best, and Ken felt a keen sense of gratitude that he had been able to contribute to a work that he knew was of great spiritual significance.

During this time Bill told Helen that he had been wondering how the spiritual theories of the Course that related to healing could be made acceptable to those practicing traditional medicine. He remarked that he had been reading articles on various subjects that he felt pertained to the matter, and among them was some intriguing information about a Russian invention called Kirlian photography He explained to Helen that this process was a form of high voltage photography that appeared to indicate the force field around matter Bill wondered whether such a device might be a reliable form of demonstrating non-physical energies through technology, thus making the subject more acceptable to the professional community

Helen said she didn't know about that, but would ask. Two days later she brought Bill information she had taken down which seemed to be some sort of an answer to that question.

"It has nothing to do with light," she said; "it's sound." And she read Bill the beginning of a transmission which was highly technical and which surprised both of them because of the scientific nature of the information.

The dictation described a device which would, when constructed, measure healing in the body Her *Notes on Sound* seemed incomplete and not totally clear, but was supplemented by images that Helen had of the device itself, which she was able to describe in her own words. Neither Helen nor Bill understood the technical aspects of the information, however, and so they decided to put the material away until such time as someone with an engineering background might come into their lives. * Meanwhile they continued their professional duties, while making little progress in healing their personal relationship.

One day, about this time, Bill was working at his desk when the phone rang. The voice on the other end of the line identified himself as a friend of one of Bill's colleagues. He was calling, he said, because he and a few associates were planning to hold a conference on the subject of Kirlian photography, and he wondered if the auditorium at Bill's hospital was available to rent. Bill told him he was quite certain it could not be rented to anyone not connected with the hospital, and so the man asked Bill if he could possibly suggest a place for holding the conference. Bill offered the first name that came to his mind—the Academy of Medicine on Fifth Avenue at 104th Street. The man thought that was a marvellous idea, thanked Bill and hung up.

Bill thought no more about the phone call until six weeks later when he received an invitation to attend the First International Conference on Kirlian Photography on a Saturday, three weeks hence. The man to whom he had spoken had written, "Thanks; please come" on the printed invitation, in obvious gratitude for Bill's help. Because of the *Notes on Sound*, Bill had a strong sense that perhaps he should attend. He asked Helen and Ken what they thought, and together they decided to ask for guidance. The answer was very clear—Helen and Ken should not attend; Bill should.

The Saturday morning of the meeting was a beautiful spring day, and Bill set off for the Academy of Medicine feeling moodily resentful about having to spend the day indoors.

"Why am I doing this?" he grumbled to himself as he headed up

---

* In the ensuing years the material has been shown to a number of eminent scientists, but no one has yet been able to supply the information necessary to construct the equipment.

91

Fifth Avenue on foot. Finally he rationalized that perhaps the reason was that he might meet one of the speakers, Douglas Dean, a professor of engineering. Bill had heard about Professor Dean and the research he had done on paranormal healing, and it occurrd to him that perhaps the professor could shed some light on Helen's healing device.

When he arrived at the Academy, he introduced himself to the conference coordinator who had originally called him about renting the hospital's auditorium.

"Is there anything I can do for you?" the man wanted to know

"Yes," Bill answered, "I'd like to meet Douglas Dean."

The coordinator introduced them immediately, and they began discussing paranormal phenomena. Since the formal part of the meeting was about to convene, they decided it would be nice to continue the conversation another time, perhaps over lunch, and they made a date to meet ten days later at Bill's office.

The Kirlian conference was then called to order, and after the welcoming remarks, the introductory talk was given by a forty-four year old lecturer and teacher of parapsychology named Judith Skutch. This was not the first time Bill had seen Judy He had attended an all-day meeting at Town Hall on parapsychology about a year before at which she was the program's chairperson. As Judy began her talk, Bill thought, "I really should meet her some time; but not today "

Chapter 7

Although Judith Skutch had been raised in a typical upper-middle class neighborhood in Brooklyn, New York, her early background could hardly have been called "ordinary."

At the age of seven, while in the third grade, the state Board of Education introduced an experimental innovative educational program for gifted children and Judy was selected as one of the participants. The program was based on the theory that self-directed education would encourage learning and creativity. Students were offered, at this early age, foreign language training, open-ended math and science programs, as well as rapid reading and typing instruction. Committee work was also encouraged, and in-depth research projects were continually being explored.

Stimulating as the program was, it also meant that for the next five years Judy was bussed to a public school that was distant from her neighborhood. Although it was a time consuming commute, her parents also insisted that she attend Hebrew School four afternoons a week, as well as Sunday School. Her father, Samuel Rothstein, an attorney, was a lay leader of organized World Jewry who had extremely deep feelings about the importance of his heritage, and he wanted to be sure his children were well versed in the meaning of Judaism.

With her Saturday mornings devoted to synagogue, with music lessons during the week and with few of her public school classmates living nearby, Judy had little time or opportunity for any kind of normal social life during her pre-teen years. As a result, books became her companions.

When she graduated from grade school the program for gifted students was continued in her neighborhood's public high school.

Part of the guidelines of the program included keeping those in the special group separate from the rest of the students, so even though she no longer had to endure a long commute each day, she still was not exposed to many people her own age who lived near her home. The enriched learning program was extremely stimulating to her though. There was very little typical classroom work; studying civics, for example, involved two-week field trips to the local courts, after which the class was not given an exam, but rather was assigned to write and publish a newspaper on all that had gone on at the various trials and procedures to which they had been exposed.

Judy's family life also could not be called typical. She grew up in a home that was extremely family oriented, and there always seemed to be a houseful of relatives in attendance. This was especially true during the late 1930's and early 1940's when so many Jews were fleeing Europe. Relatives from Nazi dominated lands who could be helped to escape the Holocaust made the Rothstein Brooklyn home their "halfway house."

With extra sleeping space needed, Judy was asked to share her maternal grandmother's bedroom. Sharing time and space with this wise woman was a beneficially powerful emotional experience for Judy, for she probably felt closer to Anna Solomon than to anyone else in the family. Her grandmother was a fiercely independent woman who had been widowed while she was in her late forties, and who was supporting herself at the time by owning and operating a progressive nursery school.

In addition to the houseful of relatives, Judy was also exposed to various spiritual and political leaders who would visit the Rothstein home to discuss matters pertaining to world Judaism with her father. Dining at the same table as Eleanor Roosevelt or with some other world reknowned figure gave Judy a grounding in social poise that was to become ever more manifest as she matured.

Most of Judy's inner thoughts were shared with her grandmother, but one she had never shared with anyone was based on an occurrence that happened when she was thirteen years old.

ᔑ *At the age of thirteen I had a spontaneous transcendent or mystical experience which touched me so much that I incorporated it into the very essence of my awareness of self. Without* understanding what the experience meant, because the intellect couldn't cope with the power of it, in some way or other I knew it was Truth.

The incident occurred when I had to have dental surgery, and was completely in the dark as to what the process involved. Not knowing that I was going to be given nitrous oxide, I was surprised to find myself strapped in a chair, with an attendant on each side of me—one to administer the gas and the other to check the progress as the surgeon was operating. When the mask was put over my face I started to fight the sensation of losing consciousness, and then in an instant was aware of a tremendous fear of 'losing myself.' The emotional pain was intense. The physical sensation was one of tremendous force, as if a pulling were occurring inside my head. It was as if I were suspended in consciousness along a line of black dots. In some way that I didn't understand, I knew that I had to progress higher, and when the outline of dots surrounded me by becoming a triangle, I knew my consciousness had to be forced through the apex of it. This I equated with death. The internal struggle was immense, but I couldn't fight it, and finally in one shearing stab of pain, I felt myself catapulted through the barrier of pain and into total peace.

There was no perception, just a feeling of beautiful, distilled absolute light. But I was not a body; I was seeing without eyes. I had an awareness of a total reality that far transcends the senses. An overwhelming feeling of well-being encompassed me, and in that place we call 'knowing' I was one with the universe—with all living souls and with God. In this state of knowing—the peace, the joy and fulfillment were beyond belief. I remember so vividly feeling the thought 'At last I'm home,' and when that occurred to me there was an echoing voice from within and all around me saying, 'now you know, now you know, now you know   ' I didn't know what I knew, but it seemed I knew All.

When I awoke from the surgery I tried to tell my mother about this beautiful incomprehensible awareness of what life really was. She listened with a smile, and said she was pleased that I had had such a nice dream. I recognized then that it would be impossible for me to translate or explain in words what I absolutely felt was knowledge.

Not being able to talk about the episode, and not having as yet the guidance to search the literature for some validation of what I had experienced, I repressed the incident until it was just bare-

95

ly part of my awareness. In fact so successfully did I repress it, that even in my college years I was not at all interested in signing up for courses that might have helped broaden my understanding of the experience. And yet somewhere deep in my consciousness, I never lost the feeling that there was a vague and mystical reality to the idea that one's true home was in the realm of total knowledge and not in the world of form. ᔰ

When Judy graduated college in 1951, she enrolled in Columbia University's School of Philosophy, matriculating toward a Master's degree in English literature. It took less than a year, however, for her to do what she and her parents had fully expected her to do—she got married. She spent the next three years working for a publishing firm where she wrote advertising copy for book jackets. This was not what she had envisioned when she was studying journalism, and it was with no regrets that she retired from the publishing business during her seventh month of pregnancy

Her first child, Jonathan, was born in 1955 and her daughter, Tamara arrived in 1959. It was Judy's experiences with the latter, when Tammy first began to talk, that nudged her subconscious into remembering quite clearly again the experience that had occurred in the dentist's chair nearly fifteen years previously .

ᔰ *Almost from the time she first began to talk, I noticed that Tammy seemed to have a sense of attunement to the world around her in a way that went far beyond the five senses. The earliest indications of this were hard-to-believe manifestations of extremely close telepathic rapport between her and me. Quite often I would have a thought, and she—from the very earliest ages of articulation—would respond to the thought I was holding in my mind.*

One day when she was about three years old, I was wondering what to make for lunch for Jonathan who was coming home from school shortly. I thought to myself that perhaps he would like tuna fish. Tammy, who was standing nearby, responded as if I had actually voiced the thought aloud, telling me she did not like tuna fish at all, and saying she'd rather I didn't make that. When I asked her, with some surprise, why she had said that, she answered, 'you said maybe you'd make tuna fish didn't you?' I recognized at that point, with a great deal of astonishment, that she was hearing in a very different way.

Throughout Tammy's early childhood these occurrences happened more and more frequently, expanding from telepathic communication to pre-cognitive dreaming and manifestations of clairvoyance. Many times she would awake from a sleep with information for me that she insisted wasn't from a dream, but was from a 'real.' She used the word 'real' because she said she could tell the difference between what seemed like fantasy and what she knew was happening. In actuality, the happenings she described had not yet happened, but were about to—as we learned after short periods of time went by.

There was the time, for instance, just prior to her seventh birthday, that she came into my bedroom early in the morning, while it was still dark outside; she was weeping unhappily, and through her tears she said that her birthday party was going to be ruined. She told me she had had one of her 'reals,' and that two of her classmates, whom she did not care for, had disrupted the party by throwing food and carrying on in such a way that their parents had to be called and asked to pick them up early. To make matters worse, the two children took their presents back before they left.

When I pointed out to Tammy that these two girls were not invited to her party, so she really need not be concerned about the dream, she recognized the truth of the statement, but still insisted the dream was a 'real.' However, the more she remembered the 'real' the more she realized that the details had nothing to do with the party. The decorations at her party were to be Mexican, while the decorations in her 'real' were from the comic strip 'Peanuts.' She also realized that the party in the 'real' was held in an apartment decorated much differently than ours. With this knowledge, she felt better and was able to go back to bed.

Tammy's birthday party was a happy affair, and nothing more was thought of her 'real' until two weeks later when she was attending the party of a friend whose home she had never visited before. I had left her at the friend's apartment building in New York City, and had told her I'd pick her up at 5 PM. At 4 PM, however, our phone rang, and Tammy, with great determination, told me I had to come upstairs to pick her up when the party was over I had no real desire to do this, but I knew that for some reason it was important to Tammy for me to do so.

When I got to the apartment, Tammy excitedly greeted me with the news that everything in the 'real' had happened just as she had experienced it. The 'Peanuts' decorations, the two disruptive children having to be sent home early—even the fact that the two children had taken back their gifts.

There were many examples of pre-cognitive dreams like this as she was growing up. Just as there were dozens of examples of clairvoyance and telepathy.

As these incidences became less and less surprising to me, I became more and more aware of how my young daughter used her abilities in a natural, constructive way, and how comfortable she was with this higher sense perception. As a consequence, I myself felt relaxed and comfortable with this capacity, and knew there was nothing to be fearful of. In fact, the personality manifestations surrounding the heightened attunement that Tammy had were all very positive ones. And it appeared to me that her paranormal traits were just an extension of her open nature.

This was particularly emphasized to me by the fact that if someone asked Tammy to perform a telepathic feat, she would not want to attempt it, and would politely decline. She told me she did not want to use her abilities unless it was for a good reason, and she thought performing was not a good reason. However, when it was important to try to send someone a telepathic message because of an emergency, she not only would offer to do so, but would usually be successful in her attempt.

This was beautifully illustrated to me one day when my uncle in New York City became suddenly ill, and my mother, who was in her car on the way to the theater, had to be informed. Tammy, who was then twelve years old, saw how important it was for me to reach my mother, and she asked me if I wanted her to send her Grandma a message. I, of course, said 'yes,' and she left the room for a few minutes. When she returned, she matter-of-factly stated, 'Grandma got it.'

I asked her how she knew, and she described the procedure, saying that she had gone into her room, stood in front of her mirror and looked intently at herself until she had 'disappeared.' Then she had said 'Grandma, call home,' three times. When she heard something 'click' in the back of her head, she said she had known her Grandma had gotten the message.

As it turned out, my mother did 'get it,' though she had no idea that she had been 'sent' anything. My father had made a stop to visit his office in order to pick up mail, and my mother, within moments of when Tammy had sent the message, said she had a feeling she ought to call home. This was contrary to all past behavior patterns, and my father, not wanting to be late for the show, tried to convince her not to waste time. There was a strong force that impelled her to make the call, however, and of course it was a helpful blessing that she did, for her assistance was urgently needed to help take her brother to the hospital.

Incidences such as this were the keystone for my growing awareness that what Tammy was evincing was a faculty for extending her consciousness beyond the parameters of her body. This somehow allowed her a far greater connectedness with people than I had originally thought possible.

In 1966, a close friend of mine, Dr Irving Rubin, who had known Tammy all her life, gave me a book. 'Here,' he said, 'I think you'll find this very interesting; it might help you understand some of the things Tammy experiences.' What he handed me was a book by Jess Stearn entitled, The Sleeping Prophet, the Story of Edgar Cayce, America's Greatest Psychic.

I brought the book home to my husband, Bob, Tammy's stepfather, and he and I became intrigued with the voluminous information written about this man's paranormal abilities. This in turn initiated a massive self-styled reading program on the subject of psychic phenomena. Bob was particularly intrigued with reading about and studying paranormal healing. It soon became evident, however, that we had to be extremely selective in choosing information that was credible. I therefore made the decision to explore the field through academic studies.

For a few years I took courses at the New School for Social Research, and was educated by some of the leading researchers in the field. My consuming interest led me to attend public programs offered by the American Society for Psychical Research and the Association for Research and Enlightenment.

Friendships soon developed with pioneer experimenters such as Dr Stanley Krippner and Dr Montague Ullman of the Maimonides Dream Laboratory in Brooklyn, New York, Dr Ian Stevenson, a well-known investigator of reincarnation at the University of Virginia's School of Medicine, Dr Lawrence LeShan, the psychologist whose lengthy and studious research resulted in a unique method of teaching psychic healing, and most of those nationally known figures who were leaders in this field. By becoming involved in their efforts, I finally realized in 1971, that my energies could best be used to help support research in parapsychology. For the more I observed the development of my daughter, and the more

I learned about paranormal research, the clearer it became to me that I was becoming completely devoted to one goal: to learn as much as possible about the total potential of the human being. For this purpose, Bob and I formed a non-profit organization which we called the 'Foundation for Parasensory Investigation.'

Running the Foundation for Parasensory Investigation proved to be an eighteen-hour a day job for Judy Skutch, for the Foundation's personnel consisted only of Judy and Bob, and he had full time employment as an investment counsellor

Because there were so many research projects that were in need of funding, Judy's time was spent talking to those seeking funds, weighing the importance of the projects, seeking advice from her many professional friends in the field, and in general helping to put people with common goals in touch with each other

The funds that the Foundation had to offer as grants were extremely modest, and initial research support was funneled through the Dream Laboratory at Maimonides Hospital, which was experimenting in altered states of consciousness. The people working there had become good friends of Judy and Bob, and when they thought a project was worth funding, Judy would try to raise the money that was needed. These were not large projects, but rather attempts to help get worthwhile research started with seed money Then, if the work showed promise, larger organizations were more inclined to offer help to continue the funding.

During this time Bob had not only started working with paranormal healing, but had also become interested in the process called "automatic writing." In the course of his delving into the latter subject he had felt the urge to experiment with the concept himself. As a result, he had been taking down material every evening in a meditative state, and the many pages of inner guidance that he had received proved of great value to him not only in his healing work, but also as a reliable source for helping him reach decisions that seemed to need more than a logical basis.

Both paranormal healing and automatic writing were among the subjects the Foundation was interested in helping to research, and Judy and Bob felt the Foundation should also help bring such subjects to the attention of the public. As a result, the Foundation sponsored a number of conferences beginning in 1973, which were open to the public.

In June of 1973 Judy and Bob organized a conference at Lincoln Center in New York that was attended by over eleven hundred people. The conference topic, "Psychic Healing: Myth Into Science," focused on the work of such people as Larry LeShan and Stanley Krippner, healers Olga Worrall and Edgar Jackson, and Sister Justa Smith whose pioneering research involved the effect of psychic healing on the stability of enzymes.

At Stanley Krippner's urging the Foundation also sponsored the first two "Western Hemisphere Conferences on Acupuncture, Kirlian Photography and the Human Aura." These were the first conferences that dealt with these matters, and the importance of them was significant enough for their proceedings to be published.

In addition, Judy kept watch over the numerous research projects the Foundation was helping to fund, including the breakthrough work in remote viewing done at the Stanford Research Institute with the Israeli psychic, Uri Geller This project, the results of which were published in the prestigious scientific British journal, "Nature," plus a mini-conference on psychic phenomena attended by sixteen world renowned physical scientists, were tremendously important in helping to get world wide recognition of the importance of investigating psychic functioning. In fact, the conference itself led to the publication of a book, *The Geller Papers,* by Charles Panati.

Judy continued taking on more and more responsibilities. She joined ex-astronaut Edgar Mitchell's Institute of Noetic Sciences as a founding member of the board; she became a faculty member at New York University's School of Continuing Education where she taught courses in experimental parapsychology and new dimensions in healing; she also accepted radio and television invitations to talk about the work she was involved in, and as if that were not enough she began her doctoral work at the Humanistic Psychology Institute in California.

Her external life thus began to resemble a company of whirling dervishes. *New Realities* magazine, in a biography accompanying an interview with Judy, described her life this way·

> "Judith Skutch's life in the 1970's can best be summarized by a typical day in her consciousness exploratorium salon in the Skutch's large New York City apartment. In one room a motion picture is be-

101

ing screened to a group interested in biofeedback. In another are seekers deep in meditation training. In still another room a medical research meeting is in progress.

Skutch herself seems to be in all places at once as she also juggles three telephones connecting people in the consciousness field to each other And at any given moment, one might find an Edgar Mitchell, a Swami Muktananda or an Uri Geller on hand, not to mention the usual assortment of psychics, mystics and physicists—or just friends of friends. To a first-time visitor, it seems a miracle that such a petite lady can keep all this going at once, in addition to often serving her home-cooked dinners to those gathered.

Just as much of a miracle, at that time in 1975, was the way Judy was able to cover up the growing emptiness and lack of fulfillment she was feeling. On the surface her life was everything she could have wanted—her work was challenging and exciting, her entire family was involved in the same interests, and her services and advice were sought by people all over the country But something vital was missing, and it was causing her tremendous emotional pain.

☙*It was also beginning to cause me physical pain, as I developed a severe peptic ulcer I well knew the effect the emotions can have on one's physical well-being, but the knowledge didn't help the symptoms at all. In fact the knowledge that I was doing this to myself made me feel even more frustrated. I searched and searched for the answers that would help me out of the prison I had built for myself, but nothing seemed to help. All I knew was that with all the different aspects of the work I was doing, there wasn't one project that didn't leave me with a feeling that the answers were incomplete—that something was missing. I respected the scientific approach, supported it, and believed it was absolutely necessary, but we were not touching at all on any spiritual aspects, even though we were aware in all of our projects—and especially in the healing projects in which we were involved—that spiritual statements were being made over and over again.*

At this time I began to have dreams that were a continuation of my earliest mystical experience. This time there seemed to be a message in them that left me with a sense of all-embracing universal love that bordered on ecstasy. But this feeling was fleeting and I could not sustain it.

The contrast between the feelings I experienced in my dreams and the feelings I had when I was awake and active was, to say the least, agonizing. And though neither my husband nor my children ever complained, I knew that my state of mind was causing our personal life to suffer

Feeling as depressed as I did, it was no wonder that I wanted to back out of a commitment I had made two months earlier I had agreed to appear as introductory speaker at a conference on Kirlian Photography that was being held at the New York Academy of Medicine, and now that the date was upon me, I desperately wanted to cancel my appearance, and yet I knew there was no way I could. And so I dragged myself across town to where the conference was being held, and gave a twenty-five minute talk on healing and the importance of bringing non-traditional healing methods into the mainstream of medical treatment.

After the conference I went straight home, and got into bed. I felt I was at the lowest point of my life. Here I had everything .   a loving husband, two wonderful, talented children, inspiring work that put me in contact with the most interesting kinds of people

and yet I felt a huge void inside as if I were splitting apart. And then in an emotional breakdown, alone in my bedroom I began to weep, and without even knowing how or where the words came from, I let out a desperate, wrenching cry: 'Won't someone up there please help me!' The words surprised me, for I had never used them before, or even had thoughts like them before.

Two days later, around nine o'clock in the morning, my telephone rang. A friend of mine from Detroit was in New York, and said it was very important that I see her, and could I possibly meet her for lunch at a mid-town restaurant. When I arrived at the appointed time she was waiting for me, and was accompanied by a man of about forty-five. She introduced him as her teacher of metaphysics, and told me he had remarkable talent as a numerologist. Knowing nothing about numerology, since it was a field that was of little interest to me, I only half listened to the stories she told me of his amazing abilities of forecasting and of helping her find a more peaceful outlook on life. After lunch, as we were leaving, my friend handed me the man's business card, and insisted that I have my chart done by him. The man looked directly at me and said 'I really do want to do your chart; it will be my gift.'

The conversation puzzled me, but I truly believed that there are no accidental meetings in life, and I felt somehow I was to comply with my friend's wishes. Rationalizing it, I told myself that numerologists, like tarot card readers and others who read the future, can be very gifted sensitives who are simply using the tools of their trade as focal points serving their talents. As such, I thought that perhaps this metaphysician was 'sent' to me to tell me something about myself that would help me resolve my stress. In my anguish, anything was worth a try.

And so the next morning I called and made an appointment to see him that afternoon. The numerological chart he had prepared, based upon my name and birth date I had given him the day before, accurately described some of the most important events that had transpired in my life. He then said I would soon meet a much older woman who would become my teacher for the rest of her life, and that within a year I would publish one of the most important spiritual documents known to humanity. When I told him that in no way was I about to write anything, he said, 'I didn't say you were going to write it, I said you were going to publish it.' I told him that was ridiculous as I wasn't in the publishing business. He smiled warmly, and merely said, 'You'll see.'

The next morning I was awakened by a phone call from my friend, Douglas Dean, who had been chairman of the conference at which I had spoken a few days before. Douglas said he had two reasons for calling me: first, he wanted to know if I were feeling better, and second, he wanted to tell me that a professor of psychology connected with Columbia University's College of Physicians and Surgeons had been introduced to him at the conference, and had invited Douglas to come up to the University for lunch the following Tuesday in order that they might discuss some topics of mutual interest. 'Would you come with me,' Judy?' he asked.

Even though I wasn't feeling well, Douglas was insistent that I accompany him. I said I would go, for though the Columbia professor had not been specific as to what he wished to discuss, I knew that for the longest time I had been extremely anxious to talk to representatives within the orthodox medical community about holistic approaches to healing. And this seemed like the perfect opportunity to present our ideas to a professional who was connected with one of the most prestigious medical institutions in the country. I told Douglas I already had an appointment for Tuesday lunch, but if the professor would make it Wednesday, I'd be delighted to join them. After I hung up, I began to think about what material I could bring along with me that might intrigue the professor enough to have him agree to help us forge some kind of link between the medical professionals and individuals who had healing abilities.

On May 29, 1975, Douglas and I drove up to the Medical Center on upper Broadway in Manhattan where we were to meet the professor—Dr William Thetford. I felt somewhat apprenhensive about the meeting, for I had no idea what sort of man to expect, since Douglas had only spoken to him for a few minutes at the conference, and had had no time to get any kind of a clue to the man's attitudes or specific interests. Douglas assured me we would find out soon enough though, for Dr Thetford had said he would be waiting in his office for us and we would go directly to lunch.

As we were walking from the car, through the flow of pedestrian traffic, we approached the crowded entrance to the Black Building at the Medical Center, and I said to Douglas, 'Oh look, there he is, waiting outside on the steps,' as I pointed to a tall slender man. Douglas was stunned. 'Yes, that's Dr Thetford; but Judy, how do you know? You've never seen him!'

I couldn't answer Douglas rationally, for I hadn't even thought through the idea before I said it. However, after I spoke the words I was engulfed by the thought that I already knew this person.

After the usual introductions, Dr Thetford said he had come down from his office to meet us so that there would be no chance of our getting lost in the maze of corridors and wings that made up the complex known as the Medical Center He then led us to the faculty cafeteria. In the lounge, he introduced us to one of his colleagues, Dr Helen Schucman, a slight, short, late middle-aged woman who couldn't have weighed much more than a hundred pounds, and who was Dr Thetford's co-worker The four of us went into the cafeteria, and after both the professors told us to call them by their first names, Bill led us to a relatively quiet table.

When the required small talk was completed, I brought up the subject I had wanted to discuss with them, but somehow neither of them showed any interest in pursuing the topic of holistic health. Bill and Helen both kept talking about research in general, and the more they talked the more I wondered what I was doing there. As the conversation continued, however, I began to feel there was something on Helen's mind that she was not revealing, *though for the life of me I couldn't imagine what it might be. All I knew was that it didn't have anything to do with the research designs she was discussing. And then, as we were eating our desserts, I heard myself saying something I couldn't believe. I turned to Helen, and out of my mouth came, 'You hear an inner voice, don't you?'*

Before I could apologize for something I seemed to have had no control over, I noticed that Helen had blanched, and there was a strained look on her face as she said, very faintly, 'What did you say?'

Bill interrupted by pushing his chair back from the table and saying, 'Why don't we all go back to our office? I think we'd be a lot more comfortable there.'

I didn't know whether or not to repeat what I had said to Helen, but I immediately became aware that it was a matter about which I didn't have to concern myself, for as Bill led us from the cafeteria, I was aware that he wanted Helen to walk with him alone, and that Douglas and I should follow them. I was also aware that they seemed to be talking intently to each other until we finally arrived at his office, where we were introduced to their associate, Dr Kenneth Wapnick. Bill then shut the door, locked it and asked quietly. 'You will keep what we say in this room confidential, won't you?'

Both Douglas and I gave him our assurances, though I couldn't guess what could possibly be such a secret.

Bill and Helen spent the next two hours telling Douglas and me the story of the past ten years. The events they described did not seem bizarre to me, and I did not feel these people were strangers. In a way I could not explain, it appeared to me as if I were being reunited with old friends, and what they were telling me seemed very natural, as though it were a continuation of events with which I had already been associated.

The entire scene was beautifully orchestrated. Here I was sitting in a prestigious medical center with people who were clearly credible in their scientific professions. And instead of discussing holistic health practices, I was holding my breath waiting to see a metaphysical document which they had scribed in secret. I asked if I might read the material.

Bill unlocked his filing cabinet and took out seven large black binders, the kind doctoral candidates use to hold their dissertations, and put them on the desk. 'Here you are,' he said; 'fifteen hundred pages. A Course in Miracles.'

I felt electrified. I reached for the binder which contained the Text, and as I opened it my eyes focused on the introduction:

This is a course in miracles. It is a required course.
Only the time you take it is voluntary

When I finished reading that first passage a great sigh of relief welled up inside of me as I heard the inner voice proclaim, 'Here is your map home.' And I knew absolutely this was the answer to my call for help. ⟨ᔕ⟩

Since Helen and Bill were scheduled to attend a staff conference that afternoon, they had to bring their meeting with Judy and Douglas to an end long before they wanted to. Before she left though, Judy said she needed to know what Bill had meant when he had said that what Helen and he were telling her was being told in confidence.

"Does this mean you don't want me to show the Course to any of my friends?" she asked.

"No," Bill said. 'We're sure the Course is not meant to be kept hidden. It's just that we don't want our names connected with it in any way"

"You see, dear," Helen added, "it would be quite awkward trying to explain to our colleagues how it all happened. Bill and I   "

Judy interrupted. "Of course. I understand."

"More important than that though," Bill said, "is the fact that this material stands completely on its own. It doesn't *need* any personalities connected with it. There are enough personality cults around already and this Course doesn't need to be the basis for another one. Helen and I don't feel we can represent this material since we don't adequately demonstrate it. As you'll see, Judy, the material is a self-study course, and Helen and I are no more than students."

When Judy returned to her apartment, she was only half-way through the door when she called to Bob, "Wait till you see what I have." She proceeded to attempt to tell him the entire story of the Course, just as it had been told to her earlier in the afternoon. Bob listened with interest, the proof of the Course, to him, would be in the content and not in the form, for he himself had been doing a kind of automatic writing for the past three years, and there was nothing

107

unusual to him in someone being used as a channel to record information of any kind. As for the content, he felt he had no particular motivation for plunging into a fifteen hundred page course at this time.

Judy started reading the Text immediately after dinner, and as she got further and further into it a surge of gratitude engulfed her, for she knew her life was about to be changed in a way that was beyond her wildest hopes. The Christian terminology of the Course did not pose too great a problem for her, since Bill had explained earlier in the day that he felt the Course used such terminology because Christianity was the dominant religion of the West, and that such language would be the easiest for most people to identify with. He had also told Judy that some of the traditional Christian language had been reinterpreted in the Course. "For example," he had told her, "the word *atonement* in the Course carries a different message than in traditional Christianity In the Course, it means the correction of the misperception that we are separate from each other and from God. *The Holy Spirit,*" he had added, "is defined as the Voice for God within each one of us. It is our guide and the link with our Creator "

It was five in the morning before Judy put down the black thesis binders and went to sleep. She had read for almost eight hours without stopping, and although she knew this was not the way the Course was to be read if one was to truly study it, she felt compelled to get as full a taste of all three volumes as she could. Without being able to intellectually explain to herself exactly how she knew it, she was certain that the Course was to be the foundation for the way she was going to try to live the rest of her life.

Before she fell asleep her mind kept repeating phrases from the Course, and she felt overcome by the truth and insight of so much that she had read. She particularly dwelled on a sentence she had read and memorized in the chapter titled "Healing and Wholeness:" "The guiltless mind cannot suffer Being sane, the mind heals the body because *it* has been healed." When she had read that, she felt convinced that the ulcer with which she had been suffering would soon become a thing of the past for her And now, just before sleep took over, she felt the absolute certainty of that knowledge.

The next morning Judy called Helen to tell her how overwhelmingly beautiful and meaningful the material was, and she asked if she and Bill would stop by on their way home, as there were a number of questions she wanted to ask them about the Course. Helen said she would be glad to drop by, and if Bill were free she was sure he would join her

And so began the first of a series of almost daily meetings that Judy had with Helen and Bill, as well as with Ken who had by this time become as integral to the welfare of the Course as both Helen and Bill. Out of these many meetings over the next three years, a feeling of deep love, connection and commitment developed among them.

Ten days after she received the Course from Helen and Bill, Judy was scheduled to go to California in order to attend some meetings related to the work of her foundation, and to have meetings with her doctoral adviser, Dr Eleanor Criswell. She asked Helen and Bill if it would be all right to take the material with her and show it to a number of her friends whom she knew would be interested.

"California's three thousand miles away," Bill said lightly "Nobody knows us out there."

The seven black thesis binders containing the fifteen hundred pages of the Course weighed almost twenty pounds, and though Judy had not taken them out of her apartment since she had received them, she had a good idea as to how heavy and cumbersome they were to carry around. When she got ready to go to the airport, the only way she could think of to carry them was in a shopping bag, but even before she picked them up she knew something had to be done to make them more portable.

On the plane she had six hours of quiet time to think about the Course and to recognize how many of her friends were going to want copies once she told them about it. She didn't have any idea how she would be able to accommodate their requests, but she remembered the very first principle of miracles in the Text, *"There is no order of difficulty in miracles,"* and she decided that if her friends were meant to have them, somehow they would get them.

One of the first people she showed the Course to was James Bolen, the editor and publisher of *Psychic Magazine*, a quality publication that was probably the most respected in its field. The magazine had a broad base of interest, and among the features they had printed were interviews with noted personalities ranging from Dr. J.B. Rhine to Richard Bach, author of *Jonathan Livingston Seagull.*

Jim Bolen naturally was interested in the manner in which the material had been received by the "scribe," but when Judy told him about the content of the Course and showed him some of the specific sections, he recognized that she had come into possession of the most unique manuscript he had ever seen—one that he eagerly wanted to become involved with on a personal level.

The problem then arose concerning *how* he could work with the Course if Judy had only one copy with her, and Jim decided the only thing to do was to make a Xerox copy Because of his publishing connections, he was able to have the job done in twenty-four hours, and for "only forty-eight dollars."

Obviously this was not going to be a very practical solution. Not only was the material in this form much too cumbersome, but Judy didn't want to lend her copy to anyone else. Yet she was absolutely certain that her professional friends who were involved in teaching and exploring the subject of metaphysics would want to study the material carefully It was then that a creative solution to the problem began to develop.

Shortly after arriving in San Francisco, Judy showed the Course to Eleanor Criswell, her doctoral adviser at the Humanistic Psychology Institute. It did not take Eleanor long to recognize the importance of the material. "An awful lot of people are going to want this, Judy," she said, "and you're going to have to make it more manageable sooner or later; you might as well do it now "

"Sure, Eleanor, but how? It costs a lot of money to put this in book form."

"It depends how you do it. I have a small publishing company called Freeperson Press, and I'm familiar with the reproduction and binding of documents. We can make Xerox reductions of the typewritten pages you have, and then we can bind them into a paper cover, and they'd be perfect for your purposes, at least for now "

"This would all fit in one volume?" Judy asked with disbelief.

"No—you'd probably need three or four volumes. And the type would end up rather small. But it would be readable."

"How much could you do it for?" Judy asked.

Eleanor said she didn't know for sure, but in limited quantities of one hundred sets, she thought the cost would be between thirty and forty dollars per set.

"That means we'd have to sell them for fifty dollars, because I'll have to give some away to people who can't afford to pay that much."

Eleanor told her that even at fifty dollars, it would be better than having to pay fifty dollars for twenty pounds of unmanageable Xerox copies.

Judy figured she had better ask Helen and Bill what they thought about the idea, and when she called them, Bill's answer was predictable: "Let's do what the Course keeps telling us to do   Let's ask."

All three of them sat quietly that evening and asked for an answer Each received the same affirmative response. In addition, it was advised that a copyright should be obtained to conform with publication practices.

And so the gears were set for printing the "first edition" of *A Course in Miracles.*

Before she hung up, Judy said that in the San Francisco area there was already so much enthusiasm for the Course and so many questions were being asked that she did not feel capable of answering, that she thought it would be extremely helpful if Helen, Bill and Ken could fly out for a couple of weeks. Bill and Helen decided it would be all right to talk informally about the Course to a few people three thousand miles from the hospital, and since they had vacation time coming, it would fit in fine with their schedule.

Judy let some friends know that Helen and Bill were coming to the Bay Area for a short stay, and that they were willing to talk about the Course to a few people. Within a week it was obvious that many were interested in coming to such a meeting, and by the time a date was set, over a hundred individuals had indicated they would attend. To accommodate them all Judy arranged to rent a public meeting room in the residential hotel where Helen was going to stay

From the very beginning of the first meeting, it was clear that the people who had been told about the Course were extremely serious about working with and discussing the material. The questions and answers went on past midnight and yet Helen showed no signs of fatigue or uneasiness. When she finally left, she said to Judy, "These people's interest is far more touching than I could have imagined."

By the end of their four week stay, they had met with over five hundred people, and it was obvious to Judy that the satisfaction Helen and Bill received from seeing how the Course affected people, more than made up for the personal anxiety each of them still had concerning their privacy

Chapter 8

The first hundred sets of *A Course in Miracles* were delivered to Judy seven weeks later There were four volumes; two were required for the complete Text, while the Workbook and the Manual for Teachers each were bound separately The volumes were the dimension of a typical paperback book—about five inches wide and eight inches long—but the type size was about thirty percent smaller than the original typed material, thus making it difficult to read. However, the Course in this form was at least easy to carry, and within a week eighty of the sets had been distributed to people in the San Francisco area, while the other twenty went back to New York with Judy

They were distributed within four days, and Judy sent an SOS to Eleanor to print another hundred. Even before they could be delivered, Judy had almost a hundred requests for the books.

It was during this time that Judy told Helen, Bill and Ken at one of their regular meetings, that she was having difficulty understanding some of the Course's terminology, and wished it had a glossary

Bill said that Helen, Ken and he had discussed this idea several times, but nothing seemed to come of it.

"Couldn't you ask the Voice for help in clarifying some of the terms?" Judy asked Helen.

Helen said she could certainly ask, but that would not necessarily mean she would get an answer "And if the answer is anything like the rest of the material—in length, that is—I'm not sure I want to hear it."

That night Helen sat quietly at home, and asked for help. The Voice returned, and what she heard was the beginning of a "Clarification of Terms" that would eventually include eleven different terms that the Course frequently used. This short section, later included as a part of the *Manual for Teachers*, took less than nine weeks to scribe.

Those nine weeks, however, were anything but peaceful for Helen. Due to a number of special meetings she had to attend, and the concomitant work connected with them, her professional environment seemed especially stressful to her

Late one afternoon she was unusually tired as she sat in her office with Bill and Ken and wearily started to read them some of the new material she had been taking down. Suddenly she stopped and began to complain about how much the Course was interfering with her life, and how much of a waste of time it was.

"You don't really believe it's a waste of time, do you, Helen?" Ken asked.

"I certainly do."

"But you know how beautiful the material is—and how meaningful it is."

"For whom?" she grumbled.

"For anyone who chooses to read it."

"Well I no longer choose to *write* it," she answered. "And I no longer choose to read it either"

Ken tried another tack. "Well, in that case there's really no point in carrying around your shorthand notebook any longer Why don't we just toss it in the garbage?" he asked as he reached across, took the notebook from her and with the expertise of a professional basketball player, looped the notebook directly into the nearby waste basket. "Well," he said as he stood up, "that should certainly simplify your life." And without waiting for an answer, he walked out of the office, with Bill close behind him.

The next morning at six-fifteen the phone rang in Ken's apartment just as he was beginning an early morning therapy session with one of his patients. He picked up the phone; it was Helen, in a panic.

"Ken, I can't find my notebook, I've looked everywhere!"

"It's got to be around somewhere, Helen; look through the papers you brought home last night."

"I've looked through them three times already," she said agitatedly; "where could it be?"

"Helen, I've got a client here now," Ken said; "why don't you   "

"Oh, my God!" they both said, almost in unison. "The waste basket!" Ken gasped.

"I forgot to take it out   I got on the phone, and   what are we going to do?"

"Call up Bill," Ken told her; "maybe he can reach the custodian."

Helen hung up, immediately called Bill at his apartment and told him what had happened.

Bill was reassuring. "Don't worry, Helen; I'll call the custodian, and tell him not to dispose of the trash till I get up there."

"How could I have done such a thing?" Helen asked as Bill hung up.

He immediately called the hospital and tried to reach the custodian. He had no luck. All he learned was that the trash was picked up every evening by midnight, and was taken to the hospital incinerator to be burned the next morning at six o'clock.

Bill hung up the phone, threw on some clothes and raced out into the street where he hailed a cab. The ride to the hospital seemed interminable, but he actually arrived in less than twenty minutes.

Although he could not locate the custodian of the building, he did find an assistant who confirmed that the man who took care of burning the trash usually did so by six in the morning, but that he had not seen him yet this particular day Bill impressed on the assistant the urgency of the matter, and the assistant took Bill to where the trash was stored prior to being burned. They opened the door, and Bill sighed with relief as he saw a whole roomful of plastic trash bags, all filled.

There must have been forty of them, and since they all looked alike, it was impossible to figure where to start searching. Bill did not relish the idea of rummaging through trash that included all kinds of leftovers from the animal research laboratories, but he knew it had to be done. He silently asked for help, and then picked two bags. The assistant opened one and dumped it upside down. Bill poked through the mess, but did not see the notebook. He helped the assistant put the trash back, and then opened the second bag. As the assistant turned it upside down, Bill spotted the notebook almost immediately, and said a silent thank you for the miracle.

As they were tidying up, the man who usually burned the trash hurried in. "Sorry I'm late," he said; "I wasn't feeling well."

That episode had a vital impact on Helen in impressing on her the true commitment she had to the Course. For she could not deny the sense of loss she felt when she thought the notebook had been destroyed.

Shortly after the third hundred sets of the paperback edition were ordered, Judy received a phone call from a friend who owned a small publishing firm, and who wanted to talk to her about the possibility of his publishing *A Course in Miracles* commercially Judy knew that no decisions about its publication—or anything else for that matter—could be made without Bill, Helen and Ken being involved. What that meant, of course, was that any proposals that were to be considered would only be decided after all four of them asked for help from their own inner guidance, or as the Course states, the "Holy Spirit."

At their next meeting the four of them sat quietly and asked. What each heard was that Judy's publishing friend should not publish the Course.

This was a pattern that was to be repeated a half a dozen times over the next three months, for as more people became aware of the Course, and as more people wanted it, more publishers expressed an interest. Judy *knew* the material *had* to be published properly, but she had no idea how it was going to get done.

The number of people who called the Foundation to speak to Judy about the Course kept increasing. Many were people she had met before, but there were just as many who were complete strangers who had heard of the books from "a friend." People whom she had not heard from in years began calling and asking how they could get the books that they had seen at "a friend of a friend's." The most bewildering part was that the number of calls was out of all proportion to the number of books that had been distributed. "The Xerox machines must be working overtime," Judy said to Bob. And still the calls kept coming from all kinds of people: psychologists, educators, ministers, business people, college students, Catholics, Protestants, Jews, blacks, whites and orientals; there seemed to be a complete universality to the demand for the Course.

In February 1976 there were no more books once again. The third hundred had been distributed to a waiting list that had nearly filled up even before the books had been delivered to Judy

When the four of them asked if another hundred should be ordered, the answer that each received was "No." They didn't understand, for the demand was obviously growing, not diminishing, and there was no other way to meet the demand than to print more of the expedient paperbacks.

"Perhaps the people who are coming to see us today are going to be the ones," Judy suggested.

The group was brought to them by John White, an old friend of Judy's, who was a well-respected author and editor As the group described their interests, attitudes and beliefs, it was obvious to everyone that here were deeply spiritual persons—ones who could shepherd the Course along its way in a responsible and dignified manner All four of them felt not only positive, but enthusiastic about the idea of such fine people being sent to them to help make the Course available in as "noncommercial" a way as possible.

They thanked John for bringing his associates, and Judy said she would get back to him after they had asked for guidance on the matter

After the group left, the four of them sat quietly together and asked if these were the people who should publish the Course.

After a few minutes they looked at each other There was disbelief on everyone's face, and without a word they knew they had each received the same answer, "No." "Only this time," they said, "let's ask 'who is supposed to publish it.'"

They sat in silence. After five minutes neither Judy, Bill nor Ken had received an answer But Helen had. She said, "I don't think you're going to like this   "

"What did you hear?" Judy asked.

"The answer was that it is to be published by those who have only the Course as their focus, and nothing else."

"That's ridiculous," Judy said. "There is no such publisher "

"Yes there is," Helen said quietly

"Who?" asked Judy

"Who published the paperback copies?"

"Eleanor did, but   "

"No," said Helen. "Eleanor printed them; the Foundation published them."

Judy's mouth dropped open. "The Foundation is supposed to

publish the books?''

"The Foundation owns the copyright," Bill interjected.

"Yes, but   " Judy was stunned. "You've heard how much it will cost. The Foundation has hardly any money "

"Let's ask where the money's to come from," Helen said.

As they closed their eyes Judy clearly heard her internal voice say, "Make the commitment first."

When they opened their eyes Judy asked what the others had heard; no one had heard anything. It was immediately clear to her that she had to make this commitment herself. Mentally calculating her current savings account, she silently pledged the entire amount to help begin this service, and informed the others of her decision.

And just as Helen and Bill had made the commitment ten years earlier to find a better way of living in the universe, so did Judy make the commitment to somehow publish *A Course in Miracles.*

When Bob came home from his office that afternoon, Judy told him what had happened. Although he had begun to read the Text in the first paperback edition, he had not been motivated to continue, and the book rested on the night table by his bed, with a book mark firmly in place at page sixty-two. Nevertheless, even though he was at this time not interested in studying the material, he completely supported Judy's involvement, and actually looked forward to seeing exactly how their Foundation was going to accomplish the task of getting the book published. Having worked in the advertising business prior to going into his present field, he knew a number of people whom he could call for advice.

Early the next morning the telephone rang, and Bob answered it. The operator's voice said there was a person-to-person call for Judy from Mexico. When Bob asked who was calling, a voice on the other end identified himself as Reed Erickson.

Bob remembered that Eric was the founder of the Erickson Educational Foundation, for whom Zelda, a friend of Judy, worked. Zelda Suplee had brought Eric to meet Judy one evening two years before, and that was the only time either Judy or Bob had met him, or even spoken to him. Bob put the phone down, and told Judy there was a long distance call from Reed Erickson.

"Eric?" She seemed puzzled as she picked up the phone, but Eric got right to the point. Zelda had sent him a copy of the original manuscript of *A Course in Miracles* a few months before, and he wanted Judy to know that his life hadn't been the same since. He went on to exclaim about the beauty of the language, the truth of the ideas and the practicality of the lessons, and said he was already studying the Course with a group of friends. He then urged that this material be published immediately, *and* in a hard cover edition with the respect it deserved. Judy told him that she and her associates had coincidentally reached the same decision just the day before, but she regretted not having enough money to publish it in a hard cover form.

"You don't understand, Judy," Eric replied. "I am calling to tell you that I was guided to sell a piece of property recently, and with the proceeds I want to underwrite the first hard cover edition of five thousand sets of *A Course in Miracles*. It must be done properly and as soon as possible."

Judy gasped in astonishment. She immediately called Helen and Bill to tell them the news.

"You see, Judy," Bill said with a smile in his voice, "there really is no order of difficulty in miracles."

When Judy met with Helen, Bill and Ken after the week-end, Helen said she felt strongly that since the Foundation was about to publish *A Course in Miracles* then the Foundation's name should be changed. "Parasensory Investigation," she said, "is misleading and inappropriate to the focus of the Course."

The thought had not occurred to any of the others, but as soon as Helen mentioned it, they each agreed that it felt as though she were right. And so the next thing to do was to ask what the Foundation's name should be changed to.

That afternoon, as they sat quietly and asked, they received no answer Judy and Bill both agreed they had heard that the name should be changed, but neither they nor Ken had received a direct answer to the question. They therefore decided they would ask again at another time.

The next day Bill called Judy to tell her that Helen had received an answer about the name the night before. She had not asked, but an image had come to her of a wrought iron entrance gate which had a plaque on it. When she looked closely, the plaque had read, "Foundation for   " and then there was a space which contained writing she could not read; after the illegible writing was the word "Peace." "I don't know what the iron gates mean," Bill said, "and neither does Helen, but we both believe that what she saw has something to do with a new name for the Foundation."

That afternoon the group met to discuss the information Helen had received. It was clear to each of them that "Foundation for Peace" was not supposed to be the name, for that seemed not specific enough. "The purpose of the Course," said Helen, "is to help you find *inner* peace." Almost simultaneously, Bill, Ken and Judy each said "inner peace," and it was clear that the new name was to be the "Foundation for Inner Peace."

* * * * * * *

The first sets of the first printing of the hard cover edition of *A Course in Miracles* were delivered on June 22nd, and that evening a party was held at Judy's and Bob's apartment. Coincidentally it was a book publishing event and a birthday—that of Douglas Dean, the professor who was responsible for the first meeting of Judy with Helen, Bill and Ken. The occasion generated amazement and disbelief at the speed with which the printing job had been completed, and at one time or another during the evening each person at the party picked up the books and seemed to fondle them gently, as though to make absolutely certain they had really been printed. When the birthday cake was brought in, Judy made a short speech of thanks for all the miracles that had happened to allow the books to be born in the way they had. Starting with Helen's images and the Voice, she went straight through the list all the way down to the miracle of how the publishing of the books had been financed. And as she held the three volumes in her hands, she—and everyone else in the room—knew without a doubt that through listening to their inner voices, *A Course in Miracles* had been beautifully guided to its perfect birth.

* * * * * * *

The first copies of the Course were sent as gifts from Reed Erickson of the Erickson Educational Foundation to over two hundred personal friends and acquaintances whom he felt would benefit by having the books. These people lived in all sections of the country, and many of them were leaders in their fields. As a result, the Course began to get excellent exposure almost immediately

Others in the group also sent out complimentary copies, and Bill sent one to Hugh Lynn Cayce, who had been so helpful to Helen and himself a few years earlier

And of course there were over two hundred names that the Foundation had accumulated, of people who had requested information about the Course; these people were informed they could now purchase the hard cover books.

Judy's schedule included a trip to California that summer When she left she took sixty-four sets with her, and had an additional sixty-four sets sent so that she would have enough books for all the people who might want to purchase them out there. She had no idea how the books would be sold, or to whom, but she knew that if she just had them available, the people who were supposed to have them would be led to them.

When Judy arrived she immediately got in touch with Jim Bolen, the editor of *Psychic Magazine*, who insisted that she lead a group discussion of the Course one evening soon. Since Bill, Helen and Ken had again agreed to spend some time in California with Judy, and since they were arriving in a few days, Judy said she thought it would be best to arrange such a discussion when the others had arrived so that they could also participate.

The group that Jim got together consisted of about twenty-five people who had been working with the material. In addition, there was a tremendous sense of dedication to the Course, and the personal stories that were told that evening about the transformations of so many relationships, was testimony to the unquestionable practicality of the principles upon which the Course is based. To Helen and Bill this, naturally, was the most rewarding aspect of the meeting that night, and of the meetings that ensued during the remainder of their stay in the San Francisco area that month. Also gratifying was the opportunity for the group to meet Reed Erickson, who was visiting San Francisco at that time. A happy opportunity presented itself to both celebrate Helen's birthday on July 14, and honor Eric for his very special role in publishing the Course.

After the first group meeting, everyone attending wanted to purchase the hard cover edition for themselves. Judy realized immediately that the one hundred and twenty-eight sets she had brought or sent out were hardly going to take care of those who wanted the books. And so the next morning she called New York, and asked to have an additional hundred sets sent.

Mail orders for the Course began to arrive at the Foundation in the middle of July, and every day Bob would open three or four envelopes containing requests for the books. It was at this time that he appointed himself head of the "mail order department" of the Foundation. This meant that after he came home from his day's work at the investment firm, he would open the mail, type the mailing labels and the file cards, and send the former to Long Island, where the books were stored and from where they were shipped. The most bewildering aspect of the whole situation to Bob was how people in areas where the Course had not been "introduced" could have heard about the books so quickly. In the first six weeks, orders came in from twenty-three different states including Florida, Texas, Louisiana, Minnesota and Washington as well as from several small towns in Canada.

Meanwhile, Jim Bolen, who had been working with the material for almost a year, recognized how deeply affecting the Course was in *his* life as well as in so many other peoples' lives, and he decided that a feature article about the Course should be written for *Psychic Magazine.*

When he had met Helen and Bill the previous summer, immediate rapport and respect were established between them. Helen, especially, showed an unusual amount of affection for Jim, and enjoyed spending time with him. However, when Jim told Helen and Bill that he would like to do an article on the Course, and would like to have them be a part of such an article, Helen's resistance was immediate. Bill recognized that Helen was reacting from fear, but he had to admit he did not have positive feelings about the idea either. Judy, on the other hand, felt that Jim's readers were just the sort who would be extremely interested in reading about the Course.

And so they did what the Course asks one to constantly do—they sat quietly and asked their inner selves if an article should be done. To Judy's suprise, her answer was, "No," and without even inquiring she knew the others had heard the same answer

Judy didn't like the answer she received, for Jim was her friend, and her "logical" mind told her that he *should* have the story written for *Psychic Magazine*. What she suggested to the others, though, was that it might be helpful if they asked again—this time asking *why* the article should not be written. The answer was very clear, and Helen expressed it most concisely

"I heard that the Course is not to be associated in any way with anything psychic," she said. "Its thrust is spiritual, metaphysical and psychological, and should not be confused with the psychic."

The clarity of the message left nothing to argue about, and although both Judy and Jim were disappointed, they each knew that the answer they had been given was correct.

During the next five weeks, Judy was asked to speak about the Course at a number of meetings that were held in the Bay area. Invitations came from adult education classes, psychology groups, spiritual organizations and from students of the Course who had formed their own study groups. As with the meeting that had been organized by Jim Bolen earlier in the summer, all of these discussions were marked by a dedication of purpose that Judy had never experienced in the previous years when she had been lecturing on subjects related to parapsychology

By the time Judy returned to New York at the end of August, almost four hundred sets of books had been ordered by mail; three or four orders would arrive every day, and while there were more requests from the California area where Judy, Bill, Helen and Ken had been, it was obvious that information about the books was spreading by word of mouth across the country An order would suddenly come from a small city in Oregon, for example, and within a few weeks other orders from that same city would begin to arrive.

Meanwhile Course in Miracles study groups suddenly began to spring up spontaneously in many parts of the country New York City, Long Island, Chapel Hill, Houston, Washington, D.C., Chicago, and both northern and southern California were some of the early locations where individuals who were studying the Course began meeting with other students of the Course in order to share experiences and help each other learn how to live by the principles of *A Course in Miracles.*

During this time Judy was receiving invitations from various groups in New York to introduce the Course. Each time she received a request she asked Bill and Helen if they would like to join her; the joint response was always a predictable "no thank you."

However, in November, when Judy was asked to talk about the Course at the Parapsychology Club of the United Nations, Bill finally agreed to go with her, saying that as long as it was a small group he didn't mind, since he doubted if any UN members had anything to do with the Medical Center where he worked.

During that same month Bill received a phone call from Hugh Lynn Cayce who thanked him for the gift set of the Course, and who said he actually felt it was one of the most important metaphysical documents he had ever seen. He went on to tell Bill that the A.R.E. book store would like to carry the books, and asked Bill if he would arrange for ten sets to be sent to Virgina Beach on consignment.

Thus was *A Course in Miracles* placed in its first retail outlet.

* * * * * * *

One of the most satisfying aspects of his job as "head of the mail room" at the Foundation, was Bob's responsibility of reading and answering the continuing flow of letters from those who had been deeply affected, emotionally, through their working with the Course. These letters came from people of every faith and background, and for the most part they recounted how, by applying the principles of the Course, various inharmonious relationships had begun to be healed. Many of the letters referred to the "miracles" that had happened when the writers began applying the lessons of the Course— miracles that helped change dramatically the direction of lives miracles that always had as their basis the newly found perception of a love that was always there.

Sometimes the letters contained truly inspirational accounts of how the "impossible" had happened, while other letters were merely to express the writer's gratitude to the Foundation for "making these remarkably practical books available."

The letters began arriving in the late Fall of 1976, and to this day they continue to arrive regularly

While Bob was taking care of the administrative work, Judy was spending a great deal of her time seeing people who had heard about *A Course in Miracles,* and who wanted to know more about it. Although requests for appointments with Judy came from individuals with all kinds of backgrounds, the majority of those she saw were psychologists, educators and the spiritually oriented. It was these kinds of people who were not only seriously interested in the books for themselves, but also for those with whom they came in contact in their professional lives. The attraction to the books by such therapists was a precursor of things to come, for as the Course spread its way across the nation there were large numbers of orders from people with these same backgrounds.

Three afternoons a week were still held sacrosanct for Helen, Bill, Ken and Judy to meet. One of the topics they discussed, on an almost regular basis, was that of Helen's continuing fear that someone at the hospital would discover what she had done, for no matter how well she knew the lessons of the Course—including lesson number forty-eight, "There is nothing to fear," she still found the idea of being discovered a great threat to her In fact, it was a tribute to her professional ability that, with these prevalent fears, she was still able to go to the hospital every day and function in a perfectly productive way

One afternoon, while they were meeting, Judy received a phone call from Jim Bolen who sounded overflowing with enthusiasm. He told Judy how the Course had helped him open up to so many new ideas that he had previously been afraid of, and that he wanted to share this great new bountiful world with his readers. He was therefore discussing with his associate the idea of expanding the scope of the magazine to include more than the psychic, and he wanted her to know that the idea he had mentioned to Judy and Bill when they'd been in California—that of changing the name of the magazine—was a distinct possibility now "Tell Bill," he added, "that the name he offhandedly suggested when we were discussing the subject, is the one we have chosen for the expanded magazine."

"You mean New Realities?" asked Judy

"That's it," responded Jim. "And we would like to inaugurate the new format with the first public presentation of *A Course in Miracles.*

When Judy, Helen, Bill and Ken got together to ask about the idea of an article on the Course in *New Realities*, the response that each received this time was an affirmative one. Helen, however, was not overjoyed, and she began to run through the familiar litany of objections she had. Bill was able to assure her though, that her anonymity would remain secure, that Jim would not print anything without their approval, and that the Course was bound to begin getting public exposure soon anyway "This way," he said, "we'll know it will be written about in a manner that will be accurate and in no way sensational."

* * * * * * *

One of the people who had started working with the Course in the fall of 1975 was Judy's friend, a 30-year-old journalist named Brian Van der Horst. Brian wrote a regular column for the *Village Voice*, a popular weekly newspaper in New York City that specialized in nontraditional news coverage and investigative reporting. Judy had met Brian in early 1975 when he had come to interview her in the course of gathering material for a story he was preparing on psychic phenomena. Although they saw each other infrequently after that, they did talk on the phone from time to time, and they had developed a close friendship.

When Jim Bolen asked Judy if she had any suggestions as to who she thought could write the *Course in Miracles* article for *New Realities*, she immediately thought of Brian. She knew that he had been working diligently with the Course and knew that he had experienced many positive changes in his relationships since working with the lessons. Although Jim did not know Brian personally, he did know of his excellent reputation as a reporter, and so he agreed to call Brian and discuss the proposed article with him.

Brian's reaction to Jim's suggestion was immediate and enthusiastic; an article on the Course was a meaningful challenge that he could really dig into and get excited about.

With Judy's help, Brian got together a list of twenty individuals—each of whom had an outstanding reputation in his or her field. Among those included on the list were educators, psychologists, business persons, authors and a medical doctor The article would

126

be written around a number of these people, and would concern itself with what effect the Course had had on their lives thus far

While Brian was beginning to do his research for the article, Jim Bolen called Judy and told her that they had decided they wanted the first issue of *New Realities* to also include a full-length interview with her

"C'mon, Jim, your magazine interviews people like Richard Bach—not Judy Skutch."

Jim explained that although she might not recognize it, her work in the field of parapsychology had made her name quite familiar to the magazine's readers, and that a separate account of the part she played in publishing the Course would be of great interest to the magazine's subscribers. He also told her that such an interview would provide an added impact to the article that Brian was writing.

It took almost an hour of Jim's most persuasive logic before Judy finally agreed that she would ask the voice within what she should do.

Judy told Helen and Bill what Jim wanted to do, and they agreed to ask with her To her surprise, Judy's answer was an emphatic "yes," while both Helen and Bill heard an equally affirmative response.

Meanwhile in the beginning of March, Hugh Lynn Cayce's organization, the Association for Research and Enlightenment, mailed out the March issue of the A.R.E. Journal. Printed in it was the first book review of the Course. It said, in part.

> The three books comprise one of the most remark-
> able systems of spiritual truth available today in the
> world of metaphysics   It is a 20th-century book
> of revelation, the scope of which is virtually without
> limit. Anyone who is searching for God, and who
> has studied the literature of metaphysics, new
> thought or the mysteries of religion East and West,
> should read A Course in Miracles.

Shortly after the review appeared, the A.R.E. bookstore in Virginia Beach sent in an order for fifty sets of books. This, Bill felt, was a signal to discuss re-printing the Course. Of the five thousand sets that had been originally printed, about twenty-five hundred remained, which would have been sufficient for the next six months or more if orders did not increase. But with the A.R.E. review, and with the *New Realities* coverage expected to have at least some effect on distribution, Bill felt strongly that another printing should be ordered.

Once again the "logical" pros and cons were discussed. Obviously no one had any idea of how much of an effect the article and the interview would have on orders, but Bill felt they could expect "a thousand or so" from the *New Realities* readers. Bob thought that was much too optimistic an estimate for a magazine that had a circulation of only fourteen thousand, and so after the usual fruitless discussion, they all asked within.

Each heard that five thousand more sets should be ordered, but Bill heard they should be ordered *immediately.*

When Bob called to re-order the books, he was told it would be three months before they could be delivered.

"That will be perfect," Bob said; "that takes us to mid-June. We won't need them till at least a couple of months after that."

Little did he know

At the end of Brian's article, the magazine had printed in a small box, information on how to obtain the Course, and five days after the issue was mailed to the subscription list, the Foundation began to be deluged with orders.

That was the signal for Bob to resign as the "one-person mail order department," and the Foundation hired a secretary to handle the correspondence and the orders, neither of which appeared as though they were going to abate.

By mid-June Bob learned they were running low on books, that the binder was having trouble at his plant, and that delivery was going to be delayed four to six weeks. There was nothing to do but process the mail and hold the labels until the second printing was delivered.

Over a thousand back orders had accumulated by the end of July when the new books were finally ready to be mailed out. No one could believe what had happened. A magazine with a circulation of just fourteen thousand was eventually responsible for over thirty-five hundred orders being mailed in over a four month period.

A third printing of seventy-five hundred sets was ordered as soon as the second printing was delivered, and it arrived in October Orders were running at the rate of twenty-five a day by then, and a number of bookstores were asking if they could carry the books. The fourth printing—ten thousand sets—was delivered in January 1978 at which time provisions were made for specialty booksellers—those that dealt with metaphysical volumes—to carry the Course.

Information about the Course was obviously being spread by word of mouth. Three months after the *New Realities* articles, orders had been received from all fifty states as well as from numerous foreign countries, including Australia, India and South Africa. In addition, the letters of gratitude arrived daily from those who recounted how the Course had "already" helped them heal relationships that they had previously thought could not possibly be healed. For Helen and Bill, that was the so-called "bottom line." The letters were their reward for the ten long years they had spent in receiving, transcribing and nurturing the material.

To this day there still has not been any paid advertising of the Course. There are, however, numerous people in various professions who now work with the Course, and who speak about it in many of the lectures they regularly give. Thus a psychiatrist may address a holistic health conference, a futurist may speak in front of governmental officials, or a psychologist may talk at a seminar on personal transformation—each describing how the Course has influenced his or her life; each thus continuing to pass along the word about, as one lecturer describes the Course, "one of the most important documents of the century "

Chapter 9

Does the story behind *A Course in Miracles* have any special meaning in itself? Or is it just another dramatic account of something extraordinary that happened to two people who might somehow have been "different" than the rest of us? The birth of the Course can truly be considered a miracle as defined by the Course itself, for it was brought to life through two people, seemingly locked into an untenable relationship, who asked for a "better way" and, joined in this goal, worked in total harmony The Course's birth then poignantly illustrates one of the Text's "fifty principles of miracles" which states, "Miracles occur naturally as expressions of love everything that comes from love is a miracle."

And there is no question that total love was the basis for this one facet of Bill's and Helen's relationship.

The Foundation for Inner Peace has received hundreds of letters from those who have recounted how their lives were changed when they began living by the principles of the Course: when they began acting out of love, rather than reacting out of fear Each letter is different. And yet each one is the same.

How does it work?

If we describe just one incident in the life of one person who is trying to live according to the principles of the Course, we might be able to see a picture of what miracles *do* mean, and what kind of miracles one can expect when one truly believes as Lesson 77 states in the Workbook for Students: "I am entitled to miracles."

* * * * * * *

In 1975, Dr Gerald G. Jampolsky, of Tiburon, California, was a fifty-year old psychiatrist with a highly successful eclectic practice. As a close associate and warm personal friend of Judy, Jerry was one of the first recipients of the Xeroxed manuscript. It came to him at a particularly appropriate time, for he had recently gone through a painful divorce and was drinking heavily He had begun to question his purpose in life, and to re-evaluate seriously his life style and values. He recognized immediately that this material could offer him a happier alternative than the road he was taking. As a result, he has been working continuously with the Course since 1975, and his professional and personal life reflect the dramatic change in him.

Jerry, as he is known to friends and patients alike, is without doubt the best known medical doctor who has done the most public speaking on the Course, and who has consistently used the principles of the Course in his professional work.

Shortly after receiving the Course, Jerry founded a non-profit organization in his home town which he named "The Center for Attitudinal Healing." At the Center, the principles of A Course in Miracles are used in helping children who have catastrophic illness shift their perception of their illness. Much of the counseling and sharing is based on lessons from the Workbook, and almost every day adults and children sit together and discuss how to release their fears in order to find peace.

One day Jerry received a phone call from a mother whose son had been in a terrible accident. She told him that her son had been run over by a tractor, had been in a coma for forty-one days, and was now, although out of the coma, completely blind and totally paralyzed except for his left arm. "Joey is terribly depressed," she said, "and we don't know what to do. Can you help us?"

"Where is he now?" Jerry asked.

"He's at home with us," the mother answered, "but he's going to be moved to a hospital in Los Angeles where they are going to try some different therapy on him."

Although "home" was over three hundred miles north, Jerry heard his inner voice say that he should see this family, and so he flew to Eureka, rented a car at the airport and drove another eighty-five miles in order to spend a short time with Joey and his parents just to determine if he could be of service to them.

131

Since the transformation of Jerry's medical practice, as well as the transformation of his whole life, is the result of his commitment to the Course, he started sharing with the family some of the concepts of the material. He discussed in detail the meaning of Lesson 108, "To give and to receive are one in truth," and he tried to impress on them the concept that helping others really helps yourself.

"Even though things may look awfully bleak to you," he told Joey, "it is always possible to find other people to help. And you'll discover," he added, "that as you find people whom *you* can help, you'll learn to help yourself.

The very next day Joey was moved to a hospital in Los Angeles, and when Jerry phoned the mother to check on the situation, she told him the doctors' prognoses were not hopeful. About ten days later, however, Jerry received a phone call from Joey's mother

"I've got to tell you about the miracle," she said, and she went on to describe how Joey had been so deeply depressed when they had arrived at the hospital that they felt he might just slip away "He was in a terrible state," she said; "nothing could cheer him up.

"I didn't know what to do," she continued. "I stood by his bed and just felt utter desolation, trying to think what I could do to help my son. And then I suddenly recalled what you told me about helping others. The only one I could think of though, was a two-year old child who was five beds away from Joey and who had been crying and crying all morning. He was obviously very ill, and the nurses couldn't seem to help him at all. In fact the child had regressed to the point where he seemed more like an infant than a two-year old. The nurses had tried walking him, patting him, everything   but nothing seemed to help, and the crying was disturbing the whole ward.

"Well, without really thinking, I went over to the crib where the child was, and without even knowing what I was doing, I picked him up and brought him over to my son's bed where I lay him, face down, screaming and crying, on Joey's chest. For an instant Joey was startled and he recoiled, but then almost immediately he lifted the only part of him that he could still move—his left arm—and he placed his hand on the child's back, and he started to stroke it and soothe it until the crying simply stopped, and the child fell asleep.

"And Joey was smiling, and the baby seemed to be smiling, and the nurses came over and looked at the two of them there lying together, and they said, 'It's a miracle; why didn't *we* ever think of this?' And within days they instituted a new program, right there in the ward, letting the children help each other The whole ward turned into a place of joy "

Unexpected? Not at all, since the Course states that "miracles occur naturally as expressions of love." The details, including the remarkable recovery eventually of Joey's speech and motor abilities, may not have been able to be foreseen by Jerry or anyone else, but the overall development was not unusual to those who study and practice the lessons of *A Course in Miracles.* For the belief system of the Course produces a state of mind where miracles are expected, because miracles are natural.

In the context of the Course one might ask "What exactly is a miracle?"

Bill Thetford's remarks have been extremely helpful to many students. He states, "The fifty principles that begin the Text are really clues to the feeling of what a miracle is. The fifty principles are a summation of what the entire Course is saying. For me, a miracle is merely the creative solution to a problem. When the Course says 'There is no order of difficulty in miracles,' it means there is no order of difficulty in problem solving. And since all problems are the result of our denying the existence of love, then a miracle can best be defined as 'a shift in perception that allows the removal of the blocks to the awareness of love's presence.' "

Those who study the Course recognize early in the lessons that what they are actually learning is how to perceive in a new way They must un-learn a system that is based on the belief in a physical reality, for the Course states that our only reality is Spirit, and our conflict comes from vacillating between the two thought systems. One belief holds we are born into bodies for a short time—to experience some joy, some pain, some happiness, some grief, and eventually death. The other belief—the Course's belief—is that we are created in our Creator's image, which is Spirit. In truth we are not bodies; we are extensions of the Thought of God. Although our natural inheritance is a state of love, we have chosen to dream that we have separated ourselves from our Source, and in so doing we think we have sinned. Based on that misperception comes all our

133

guilt, and out of guilt comes fear We can learn to release this fear and undo our mistaken sense of sin and guilt only through the practice of forgiveness, for it is by forgiving others that we learn to forgive ourselves, and thus our illusions of separation can be healed. As the Course states, "All healing involves replacing fear with love."

* * * * * * *

Was the Voice that Helen heard dictating the material really that of Jesus? Both Helen and Bill believed the material must stand on its own, regardless of its alleged authorship. At her deepest level, Helen was certain that the Voice was that of Jesus, and yet she still had ambivalent feelings on the subject.

Having no belief in God, I resented the material I was taking down, and was strongly impelled to attack it and prove it wrong. On the other hand I spent considerable time not only in taking it down, but also in dictating it to Bill, so that it was apparent I also took it quite seriously. I actually came to refer to it as my life's work, even though I remained unconvinced about its authenticity and very jittery about it. As Bill pointed out, I must have believed in it if only because I argued with it so much. While this was true, it did not help me. I was in the impossible position of not believing in my own life's work. The situation was clearly ridiculous as well as painful.

But where did the writing come from? Certainly the subject matter itself was the last thing I would have expected to write about, since I knew nothing about the subject. Subsequent to the writing I learned that many of the concepts and even some of the actual terms in the writing are found in both Eastern and Western mystical thought, but I knew nothing of them at the time. Nor did I understand the calm but impressive authority with which the Voice dictated. It was largely because of the strangely compelling nature of this authority that I refer to the Voice with a capital 'V ' I do not understand the real authorship of the writing, but the particular combination of certainty, wisdom, gentleness, clarity and patience that characterized the Voice makes that form of reference seem perfectly appropriate.

At several points in the writing the Voice itself speaks in no uncertain terms about the Author My own reactions to these

134

references, which literally stunned me at the time, decreased in intensity until they reached a level of mere indecision. I do not understand the events that led up to the writing. I do not understand the process and I certainly do not understand the author ship. It would be pointless for me to attempt an explanation.''

* * * * * * *

When *A Course in Miracles* began to come through Helen, no one could foresee what effect it would have on the world. But it seems clear that this material was given to Helen and Bill for a broader purpose than to help just two people find a "better way" to live in the universe. It has already affected too many lives in a positive way for it to have been given for such a limited reason. And so it appears that in its own time, and in its own way, it will spread to wherever it is needed.

The concepts of the Course are such that anyone who studies the material seriously *must* find that his or her perceptions are changing   that when one believes and follows the spiritual reality that the Course presents, then only peace of mind can be the result. For when we release all of our fears we will be and feel what we really are in truth, which is total love. And then we will *know* that the journey to God has truly been a journey without distance.

Afterword

In 1977, at the age of 68, Helen had to retire from the hospital, having remained on the staff two years past the standard retirement age. Less than four years later, on February 9, 1981, she died in New York City

The following year, as a testimonial to Helen, the Foundation for Inner Peace published *The Gifts of God*, the complete collection of Helen's poetry, which she had written between 1971 and 1978. Although the poetry was not scribed exactly the way the Course was, many of the poems have the same inspirational quality as the Course.

In 1978 Bill took early retirement. He moved to California where he was involved in private counseling, and also helped write and edit several books with Jerry Jampolsky He died of a sudden heart attack on July 4, 1988.

Judy moved to California in 1978. Her time is mainly focused on bringing to fruition numerous translations of the Course.

In 1983 Ken formed the Foundation for *A Course in Miracles*, which is devoted to teaching the principles of the Course. His foundation is located in Temecula, California.

Students of the Course continue to form spontaneous, autonomous groups that meet regularly to discuss and study the material. The Foundation for Inner Peace has no way of knowing how many of these groups actually exist, but it is believed that there are more than two thousand throughout the world.

As of the spring of 2001, fourteen foreign translations are being worked on. The Spanish edition was published by the Foundation for Inner Peace in 1993, the Portuguese edition in 1995, and the Russian and Chinese editions in 1999. In addition, the German edition was published in 1994, the Hebrew in 1996, and the Italian and Dutch in 2000. All are available from the Foundation.

*A COURSE IN MIRACLES can be obtained
for forty dollars through:*
     The Foundation for Inner Peace
     P.O. Box 598
     Mill Valley, CA 94942
(A single volume/three-in-one edition, printed on Bible
paper, is also available. As of January 1996: softcover, $28
or hardcover, $30.)

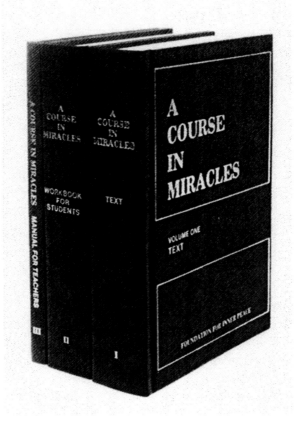

Robert Skutch's latest books, THE DAY
CONGRESS REMEMBERED and WHO'S
IN A FAMILY? were both published in
1995. He has also written for radio and
television, and currently lives in northern
California.